The Millenniu

and the

Book of Revelation

For Myrtle

The Millennium

and the

Book of Revelation

R.J. McKelvey

The Lutterworth Press
Cambridge

The Lutterworth Press
P. O. Box 60
Cambridge
CB1 2NT

e-mail: **publishing@lutterworth.com**
website: **http://www.lutterworth.com**

British Library Cataloguing in Publication Data:
A catalogue record is available from the British Library

ISBN 0 7188 2996 4

Printed by
Redwood Books, Trowbridge

CONTENTS

PREFACE

This book is an attempt to understand the meaning of the millennium in the Book of Revelation and what it has to say to us today. Revelation is a strange book and how one should understand the thousand-year reign of Christ and his saints is not at all clear. However, that has not deterred people from making predictions about the millennium and founding millenarian movements. The hope that one day Satan will be bound and the forces of evil contained so that Christ and his followers reign undisturbed on earth has captured the imagination of visionaries, artists, musicians and revolutionaries.

In the early church the millennium was understood as Paradise on earth. The materialistic interpretation it was given shocked Augustine of Hippo and he gave it a completely new meaning by spiritualising it. But the hope of an earthly kingdom reasserted itself and grew throughout the Middle Ages. It generated powerful movements of reform on the continent from the time of the Reformation. Its association with the hope of the Second Coming of Jesus Christ made it a potent force in the nineteenth century until it was discredited when successive dates set for the End were not fulfilled. Today the mainline churches no longer build their hopes upon specific biblical prophecies and the millennium has little or no part in their thinking on the future, whilst various Christian groups and other religious or quasi-religious sects create apocalyptic scenarios for the year 2000. Part One of this study is a survey of the better-known and more influential millenarian thinkers and movements. Included in this section is a study of the influence which the millennium had on Christian missions.

Secular versions of the millennium have made their appeal throughout history. Some of these owe their origins to religious motivation. Others explicitly reject all association with religious belief. The Nazi doctrine of a thousand-year state ruled by the Aryan elite and the Communist promise of a happy and classless society are examples of secular millennialism. Their impact on world history has led historians and sociologists to study earlier movements. I do not attempt to look at secular millenarian movements; numerous studies are available.

In recent years the Book of Revelation has been the subject of a good deal of scholarly attention. This provides us not only with essential background material for understanding the millennium but shows that the millennium is integral to the whole of Revelation. A study of Revelation is therefore essential to understanding the millennium. We shall find that the millennium is a specific response to a specific situation. It is the promise made to those who engage in the demanding business of bringing the gospel to bear upon the dominant ideology. What John's millennium has to say to us about God's concern for those who are unjustly treated and the church's task today is considered in Part Two.

The conviction that the Book of Revelation has something vital to say to today's world grew within me when I was engaged in training ordinands in South Africa during the apartheid era. The critique of the ideology underpinning apartheid worked out by liberation theologians and John's critique of the ideology which maintained Roman rule fused together to become a highly subversive message. Since returning to Britain I have been reading Revelation in a very different context, but John's critique challenges me afresh. In the following pages I attempt to say what I believe the book says to us today.

Recent writers on Revelation to whom I am particularly indebted are David Aune, Richard Bauckham, Adela Yarbro Collins, Elizabeth Schüssler Fiorenza, Christopher Rowland and John Sweet. My conversations and correspondence with Richard Bauckham were a great help. Christopher Rowland's writings helped me both in understanding the text of Revelation and its connections with today's world. I am grateful to my friend and former colleague, Roger Tomes, for reading the typescript, checking references and making many helpful comments. My thanks are also due to my neighbours, Norman Leak and Frank Saunders, for their assistance. Last but by no means least I am greatly indebted to my wife, Myrtle, who has helped me in all sorts of ways, particularly on the computer.

R.J. McKelvey

INTRODUCTION

Millennialism, or millenarianism, is essentially about hope. It is the refusal to accept that things need be the way they are and cannot be changed for the better. It predicts a happier future for the human community on earth. In other words, millennialism is an ideology of change. For that reason it has evoked great interest among historians and sociologists as well as theologians, quite apart from the expectations which are being created by the approach of the year 2000.

The Latin term *millennium* literally means a period of one thousand years. Its use is based on Jewish and Christian interpretations of the utopia. The term millenarian (or *chiliastic*, the Greek equivalent) is used nowadays in a wider sense to include movements which expect total and collective salvation or liberation. Scholars debate the influences that contribute to millenarian movements. Students of the Book of Revelation have not been in the habit of looking beyond the text for the origin of John's vision, but the sociological approach to the New Testament has made it clear that the multiple causes that historians and sociologists now recognise as contributing to millenarianism are to be seen in John's vision.

Interpretation of the millennium in the Book of Revelation has been influenced to a great extent by the connection which students and scholars have made between the millennium and the Second Coming of Jesus Christ. The descent of the Word of God, i.e. Christ, to earth, described in Revelation 19.11-21 is taken to be the Second Coming elsewhere described in the New Testament. This event is then taken along with the millennium passage in chapter 20 as a single sequence: Christ returns to earth, Satan is locked up and Christ and the saints reign for one thousand years. This interpretation, in which the Second Coming takes place *before* the millennium, is known as premillennialism. The advantage of this view is that it follows what appears to be the natural order of events in Revelation. Moreover, it can claim to be the interpretation held by the early fathers of the church.

Postmillennialism by contrast holds that Christ will not return until *after* the millennium. According to this view the earth must first be prepared for his coming. Some who hold this view have interpreted it in a spiritual way, emphasising evangelism and the spreading of the gospel and Christian teaching throughout the world. Others have understood preparation for the millennium in terms of social betterment and the benefits resulting from responsible government. This interpretation was anticipated by the twelfth-century theologian Joachim of Fiore. His teaching on the dawning of the new age of the Spirit can be said to have prepared the way for the confidence in historical progress in the eighteenth and nineteenth centuries that flowed from the Enlightenment. The postmillennial view has suffered from the loss of confidence and the questioning of progress in today's world.

These contrasting views indicate a significant theological difference. The premillennialists believe that it is God and God alone who acts to bring in the kingdom whereas the postmillennialists believe that he uses human agents to do so. The former think that the latter underestimate the power of evil, while the latter believe the former take too pessimistic a view of the world.

In addition to premillennialism and postmillennialism we have to take note of amillennialism. This is the interpretation popularised by Augustine. The term amillennial is misleading, for it gives the impression that Augustine rejected the doctrine of the millennium. He actually affirmed it but declared that it had in fact begun with the coming of Christ at his incarnation. Christ would come again, after the thousand years. This interpretation won wide appeal and still has supporters. It has advantages over premillennialism. By spiritualising the millennium it emphasises the symbolic nature of the Book of Revelation. It fits more easily with the teaching of the New Testament on Christ now reigning as Lord and believers raised up with him and sitting in the heavenly places (Eph. 2.6; Col. 2.12; 3.1). Its serious weakness is its emptying the millennium of its strongly eschatological and futurist character.

It has to be said that interpretation of Revelation has been made unnecessarily difficult by finding in the book a connection between the millennium and the Second Coming of Christ. We shall see that in Revelation the millennium is not an adjunct of the Second Coming but stands in its own right.

The subject of the millennium introduces us immediately to the highly symbolic nature of the Book of Revelation. It is unfortunate that scholars who are aware of the need to interpret the book symbolically frequently fall into a literalistic mode when they come to the millennium. Once the millennium is taken literally, as predicting an actual period in the future history of the human race, all sorts of questions follow: When will the millennium be? Where will it take place? Who are the nations whom Satan deceives after the millennium ends? (Bauckham, 1993b, 108). This means to think of the millennium in terms of premillennialism and postmillennialism is to focus on the wrong questions. To ensure that we address the correct questions we have to begin by paying attention to John's intention in writing his book.

Quotations from the Bible are taken from the New Revised Standard Version unless otherwise indicated.

PART ONE

MILLENNIAL HOPES

I
The Ups and Downs Of Millenarianism

Early Church Fathers

The early church believed widely in a millennial kingdom on earth. Papias, Barnabas, Justin Martyr, Irenaeus, Tertullian, Hippolytus, Commodianus, Victorinus and Lactantius all looked forward to it (Bietenhard, 1953). Justin Martyr (*c.*100-165) is typical: the saints will be resurrected and live in peace and prosperity for one thousand years in a restored and greatly enlarged Jerusalem (*Dialogue* 80-81). The early writers were agreed that the Second Coming of Christ would take place before the millennium but differed in the sequence of events leading up to the End. Some expected the New Jerusalem to descend to earth at the start of the millennium, others at the end of it, when the new heaven and the new earth would also appear. But all of them believed that the millennium would be a time of unprecedented material and spiritual well-being and happiness. There is no doubt that the appeal of an earthly millennium of peace and prosperity to the early church had something to do with the persecution it suffered. People found in Revelation the encouragement and strength to endure and die for the cause of Christ. Irenaeus declared that the reason why the millennium is necessary has to do with the fact that it promises the faithful their reward on the very scene of their suffering (*Against Heresies 5.32*).

The belief that Christ would come before the millennium, i.e. the premillennial view, was held by all the early church fathers. It marked the beginning of a tradition that still persists. The premillennialism of the early church has come to be known in some quarters as classical millennialism. This is to distinguish it from later premillennialism which is dispensational (Gilbertson, 1997, 9-13).

The Montanists

The Montanists were particularly strong on millenarianism. Montanus began prophesying in Asia Minor in the second half of the second century. He and his female assistants taught that the New Jerusalem was about to descend to earth. The site for the heavenly city was far removed from populated areas, on a plane near the village of Pepuza in western Phrygia. There the prophet led his followers to prepare for the great event. They formed a strange company in that remote spot. All earthly ties were severed and new ones were not permitted. Wives and private property were renounced, and in a strict ascetic regime the Montanists waited for the new age. Tertullian joined them and also looked for the millennium and the New Jerusalem on earth (*Against Marcion* 3.25). The New Jerusalem did not appear, but with humanity's inborn ability to make the most of things these apocalyptic visionaries settled down to life in a city of their own making.

The fact that belief in the millennium was held by the Montanists and their predictions had been discredited made the church suspicious of the doctrine. We find Origen (*c.*185-254) reacting against the literal interpretation of the New Jerusalem (*de prin.* 2.11.2). But it was not only Montanist influence and the literal and sensual way in which the millennium was understood which caused it to be called in question. Great changes were taking place in the fortunes of the church as a result of Constantine having become emperor and Christianity made the favoured religion. Understandably, Christians grew less inclined to view Rome as the Beast of Revelation. New interpretations of the millennium began to appear.

The Millennium Reinterpreted

A novel way of understanding the millennium was started by Tyconius (late fourth century) (Bietenhard, 28-29). A lay member of the breakaway Donatist church, Tyconius suggested that the millennium referred to the present age, in which God helps the saints so that they are not overcome by evil. The millennial rule of the church would last until the Second Coming of Christ. This interpretation was followed by Augustine.

Augustine (354-430), who had begun by subscribing to the traditional understanding, reacted against its crude materialism. He proceeded to spiritualise the millennium along the lines set out by Tyconius. According to Augustine Satan is bound for the period from the birth of Christ to his Second Coming, which corresponds to the period of the millennium (*City of God*, 20.7-17). The New Jerusalem is already present; it descends to earth whenever grace changes the human heart and makes one a citizen of the heavenly city. This equation of the thousand-year reign of Christ and the saints with the life of the church on earth in the present age helped prepare the way for what later became known as amillennialism, i.e. no future millennium. Augustine, however, believed in the millennium (the present era) and still expected the return of Christ, so he is more correctly a postmillenarian (Wainwright, 1993, 38). Augustine's great influence led to the hope of a future millennium being rejected by the church. The Council of Ephesus in 431 condemned future millennial predictions. Augustine's interpretation of the millennium became the official view of the church for much of the Middle Ages.

Other influences were now at work. The transformation in the church's fortunes from the time of Constantine and the advent of the Holy Roman Empire had a decided effect on millenarian thinking. Moltmann describes the "Thousand Years' empire" as political millenarianism. "The church's theology turned into an imperial theology, because it was no longer just Christ's church which represented God's rule on earth; it was the Christian emperor and the Christian empire too" (1996, 154). This was another example of the historicising the millennium; the difference was that the millennium was believed to be embodied in earthly institutions.

Hope of an Earthly Millennium Reasserts itself

But the doctrine of a future earthly Paradise was not dead. It made a number of remarkable reappearances. The hope of a millennial kingdom at Jerusalem after Christ's return was a powerful motive at the beginning of the crusades (Cohn, 1957, 40-52). The expectations created by the year 1000 and the millennium of the passion of Jesus in 1033 were still running so high (Glaber, 2-4, ed. France, 1989) that Peter the Hermit could use prophecy to recruit great numbers of people for this crusade (1095).

Nobles like Godfrey of Bouillon and Raymond of Toulouse were invested with a messianic aura. Many hoped for the Emperor of the Last Days, who would overthrow the power of Islam, convert the Jews and inaugurate the age of bliss in anticipation of the End. They looked for a new Charlemagne, the heroic champion of Christ, to fulfil this role. Later they put their trust in Louis VII of France. They were less interested in the Pope Urban II's aim of assisting the Christians of Byzantium than in capturing and occupying Jerusalem. The Holy Land was their promised land. The Jerusalem that obsessed their minds was more than a purely historical and terrestrial reality. It was the symbol of the heavenly Jerusalem which, according to the Book of Revelation, was to replace it in the last days (Cohn, 44-45; Breders, 1984, 79-80).

Joachim of Fiore

The power of the millennium as a future hope to reassert itself was expressed in a remarkable way in the writings of Joachim of Fiore (1132-1202). He recovered the eschatological millennium and influenced the church's thinking for centuries to come (Reeves, 1976, 124-125, 157; McGinn, 1985, 154). Basic to Joachim's thought is the idea of three eras of history: the age of the Father (the Law of Moses), characterised by fear and servitude, the age of the Son (the gospel), characterised by faith, and the age of the Spirit characterised by love, freedom and joy. The third age would be the millennium, which would come between 1200 and 1260. The millennium, according to Joachim, would be like the Sabbath, a time of rest for all. There would be no wealth or poverty; everyone would live in voluntary poverty. No one would need to work because everyone would have spiritual bodies and not need food. Church and state would give way to a community of perfected beings who would not require the help of clergy or sacraments. This kingdom of the saints would endure till the Last Judgement.

Many sought Joachim for his insights into prophecy. Richard the Lionheart asked his advice concerning the Third Crusade. More significantly, Joachim's ideal of a totally unworldly society enthused the rigorist wing of the Franciscan Friars, the so-called Spirituals. They appropriated his prophecy to themselves. Like many other religious orders, the Spiritual Franciscans saw their calling as embodying the true spiritual life of the future and leading the world towards it. But for the purposes of our study Joachim's importance lies in the fact that he reinstated the Book of Revelation as a prophecy of future events. This was to have a profound influence for centuries throughout Europe (Bloomfield and Reeves, 1954). The significance of Joachim's influence is all the greater when it is remembered that the official teaching of the church was amillennial and Joachim had been condemned by the Lateran Council (1215).

The thirteenth century saw millennialism take a form which was to express itself strongly in the coming centuries when Joachim's ideas were given political expression during the rule of Holy Roman Emperor, Frederick II (1194-1250). Frederick became the emperor of the Last Days. For one who saw himself as God's Messiah, commissioned to restore peace and usher in the millennium, it was inevitable that a conflict should develop between Frederick and the Papacy. Whereas Germany regarded Frederick as its saviour, Italy turned him into the Beast of Revelation. Frederick died suddenly in 1250, a decade before he was to have assumed his eschatological role. But the seeds of political radicalism had been sown and would produce a wild harvest (McGinn, 1979, 168-179).

Chrsitopher Columbus

Fascinating evidence of the widespread influence of eschatology on Europe during the Middle Ages is found in the writings of Christopher Columbus (1451-1506). Historians nowadays believe that Columbus' achievements resulted not only from his skills in seamanship, navigation and astronomy but from his interest in spreading Christianity and the influence Joachim of Fiore and the Franciscans had upon him (Watts, 1985; Flint, 1992).

In 1498, near the island that Columbus named Trinidad, the explorer located another island, or what he took to be an island. It was in fact a continent. The enormous volume of fresh water pouring into the Gulf of Paria (actually water from the delta of the great Orinoco river of present-day Venezuela) led Columbus to believe that he had come upon the rivers mentioned in Genesis 2.10-14. The fresh water, temperate climate and luxuriant vegetation convinced Columbus that he had found Paradise. (The ancients believed Paradise was in the east; Columbus thought that he had reached it by travelling west.) "God made me the messenger of the new heavens and the new earth of which he spoke in the Apocalypse of St. John . . . and he showed me the spot where to find it" (quoted by Watts, 102).

This extraordinary claim by Columbus has been attributed to physical or neurotic illness by some scholars, but it is defended by others. They believe that Columbus was fully in possession of his faculties in making this claim and was writing with an eye on the continued patronage and financial support of his king and queen (Flint, 180; McGinn, 1979, 284). Whatever one may think of Columbus's use of the Bible and the apocalyptic traditions as a means of underwriting his ambitious schemes, what he says about the millennium is evidence of the power of its appeal during the Middle Ages. More important still, his New World was to exert an irresistible millenarian attraction for many who came after him. Before we consider this we have to take note of a new form of millenarianism in Europe.

Militant Millennarianism

Millenarianism of a militant kind appeared in Bohemia with the Taborites in the early years of the fifteenth century (Cohn, 221ff.). They were an extreme group of followers of the reformer John Huss and took their name from Mount Tabor, the mountain where they believed Christ had predicted his coming again. They emerged from the long struggle between the Czechs and the Catholic and largely German ecclesiastical hierarchy and the movement for reform led by Huss. Bitterly critical of corruption in church and state, the Taborites declared that it was time to abolish all evil in preparation for the millennium. They believed it was the duty of the elect to rid the world of sinners. The cleansed earth would receive Christ who would return in majesty and rule the saints. Under the brilliant military leadership of John Zizka the Taborites defeated the much superior imperial army sent against them, but after Zizka's death and a split in the movement the remaining radicals were defeated in 1434.

Germany during the period marked by the Reformation was fertile ground for millenarian ideas. A militant form appeared with Thomas Müntzer (1490-1525) (Cohn, 251-271; Matheson, 1988, 230-252). Influenced by Martin Luther, Müntzer broke away from Catholic orthodoxy, but followed Joachim's ideas and was soon in fierce conflict with Luther. Whereas Luther had difficulty in becoming enthusiastic over the Book of Revelation, Müntzer seemed to talk about nothing else. What he had learnt from Joachim of Fiore was gradually turned into a radical programme and used to legitimise a revolution.

Müntzer's fiery denunciations of those who oppressed the poor (and of Luther, for colluding with the oppressors) and his virulent pamphlets got him into serious trouble with the authorities. But undeterred, he worked out his doctrine of social revolution. The Peasant Revolt in 1524 was the opportunity he was looking for. Although the revolt did not lead to the apocalyptic struggle that Müntzer had predicted, it was catastrophic. Many thousands of peasants perished, and Müntzer himself was executed. But his influence lived on.

Revolutionary millenarianism expressed itself fiercely among the mass of the unemployed and desperate foreigners who gathered at the city of Münster as a result of the preaching of militant Anabaptists in the early 1530s (Goertz, 1996). John Matthias arrived from Holland, declaring that the righteous must take up the sword and actively prepare for the millennium. By 1534 the Anabaptists, under Matthias, had taken control of Münster in an armed uprising. They declared that Münster was the New Jerusalem and proceeded to condemn to death everyone whom they considered ungodly. Lutherans and Roman Catholics alike were targets of the frenzied mob, and those who did not flee were forcibly re-baptised. The so-called New Jerusalem became a killing field. Alarmed by the uprising, government forces, led by the Bishop of Münster, went to the attack. After a bitter struggle Matthias's theocracy ended in terrible bloodshed in June 1535 (Hamilton, 1981, 12-17).

Martin Luther and John Calvin

Such fanaticism and the discrediting of millenarianism help us to understand why Luther and Calvin did not show any great enthusiasm for the subject. Luther was frank about his difficulties with the Book of Revelation in the terse Preface to the first edition of his German translation of the New Testament (1522). But faced with Rome's obduracy and Müntzer's fanaticism, the Reformer considered it wise to write a new and considerably longer preface (1530) in which he deleted critical comments and provided an introduction to the meaning of Revelation (*Works,* 35, 399ff). Now he had no hesitation in using Revelation in his polemic against the papacy. Luther's interpretation was followed by Protestants for centuries to come, both on account of his identifying the Pope as the Antichrist and because this identification was placed within an historically progressive interpretation of Revelation. Thus, although the Lutheran Augsburg Confession (1530) denounced those "who are now spreading Jewish opinions to the effect that . . . the godly will take possession of the kingdom of the world" (1.17), Luther's use of Revelation as prophecy of what has yet to happen helped the revival of interest in the millennium.

John Calvin distanced himself from apocalyptic speculation. He dismissed the future millennium and upheld Augustine's interpretation as the doctrine of the church's life here and now (*Institutes* 3.25.5). But this did not deter Calvin's followers from affirming belief in the millennium as a future hope. It was a Calvinist from Germany, Johannes Heinrich Alsted (1588-1638), who produced one of the most influential treatises on the millennium (Clouse, 1979, 189-207). The horrors of the Thirty Years' War and the predictions of Revelation led Alsted to believe that the End was near. As he pored over the prophecies of Daniel and Revelation he came to the conclusion that he had to abandon Augustine's interpretation in favour of a future millennium. Alsted traced the history of the church in John's visions of the seals, trumpets, and bowls, and calculated that in the year 1694 the papal power of Rome would collapse and the millennium begin.

II
Millenarianism Grows Apace

Millenarian Movements in England

What was happening on the continent soon began to appear in England. Belief in a future millennium grew apace. Joseph Mede, the distinguished Fellow of Christ's College, Cambridge (1586-1638) was strongly influenced by Alsted. Mede's writings on the millennium marked a definite break with Augustine's view since they set out the thousand-year reign as a distinctive period of history that was still to happen (*Works*, 2. 747-51). Mede developed the theory of synchronism, which was a version of recapitulation, explaining different passages of Revelation as descriptions of one and the same event. Thus the millennium, in his view, corresponds to the vision of the countless multitude (7.9-14) and the New Jerusalem (21-22). The millennium would be marked by the downfall of the Turks, the conversion of the Jews, the end of the papacy, and the resurrection of the saints and martyrs.

The doctrine of a future millennium was eagerly adopted by the English revolutionaries in the 1640s. Mede's Latin treatise was translated into English by order of the government. But whereas Mede thought of the millennium in strictly religious terms as the flowering of Protestantism, the Puritans gave it a definite political character. The Antichrist was now associated not only with the Pope but also with Archbishop Laud and the secular power of the monarchy. Theological speculation was fuelled by other things. Bad harvests, epidemics and rising prices hit the poor severely. Harsh treatment of the poor in the courts of the land spurred the Levellers to campaign for a social contract. Along with equality of all before the law, they included freedom of conscience, religious toleration and, above all, a better deal for the poor and the working classes. Their motivation was strongly biblical and religious. Even if pamphlets like John Lilburne's revolutionary *Free Man's Freedom Vindicated* (1646) do not specifically mention the Kingdom of God, they do show how clearly the Levellers were working for a new and godly rule (Brailsford, 1961, 119-120).

Millenarian ideas influenced the Diggers (Hill, 1975). Viewing themselves as the "true Levellers", this small group of impoverished men and women got its name from the fact that it began by digging up waste land for gardening purposes (1649). They believed that private property had corrupted humanity and planned a millennial kingdom of social equality, planting vegetables to feed the hungry. Unhappily, local harassment and harsh weather took their toll and the community collapsed. Its inspirational leader, Gerrard Winstanley, grew pessimistic and eventually gave up millennial hopes.

But millenarianism was a dominant force and the Puritans looked for the Second Coming and the millennial kingdom (Toon, 1970). From studying the prophecies of Daniel and Revelation, they pointed to the four great empires of history (Assyrian, Persian, Greek, Roman). The last of these (the Holy Roman Empire) was visibly staggering to its doom. Soon the fifth era – the so-called Fifth Monarchy – would begin (Dan. 2.44) (Rogers, 1966). The saints would prepare the way and Christ would return to reign for a thousand years. The movement, which started among the artisans of London and began by supporting Oliver Cromwell, combined the expected theocracy with strong republican sentiments. Supporters of the movement in the New Model Army went so far as to claim that Christ had already appeared in the army. Others believed that the saints in the army should prepare for the Second Coming. Their militancy worried many. Cromwell was alarmed. John Milton roundly dissociated himself from their worldly understanding of the Kingdom of God. In *Paradise Regained* he declared that the fulfilment of the millennium prophecy must await God's good time. Disappointment reigned when the Protectorate was established. The Fifth Monarchists felt that their hopes were dashed and turned against Cromwell. Gradually, English millenarianism became associated with increasingly narrow and sectarian forms of radicalism. Instead of revolutionary millenarianism, there appeared quietistic and moderate interpretations of the Book of Revelation that did not pose a threat to the state. Fanatics like the Muggletonians and Joanna Southcott only served to bring prophecies on the Book of Revelation into disrepute and contempt (Harrison, 1979).

Millenarianism in New England

Before we consider the resurgence of millenarianism in England at the time of the French Revolution we need to look at the remarkable vitality of the phenomenon in North America. There it expressed itself in its postmillennial form. Millennial teaching was taken to New England by the Puritans and German and Dutch pietists, survivors of the great revolutionary uprisings of the fifteenth and sixteenth centuries. They believed themselves called by God to help establish his kingdom in a virgin land and thus demonstrate to the decadent nations of the old world the possibility of a Christian society. It was the Great Awakening, a series of revivals between 1725 and 1760, however, which did most to foster millenarianism and help it spread from New England to the rest of the colonies. The Presbyterian Jonathan Edwards (1703-1758), whose powerful preaching contributed to the Awakening, interpreted what was happening as a sign that the millennial utopia of peace and well-being would soon arrive, followed by the Second Coming of Christ. Edwards declared that the millennium would very likely begin in America (*Works*, 4. 353-358). He criticised the government of Massachusetts for not encouraging the revivals, warning that the time was coming when the saints would rule the earth and possess full authority (4. 373). Although millenarianism in North America owed something to increasing economic inequality, demographic pressures, the rise of a commercial and secular culture, and, indeed, the beginnings of American nationalism, it was not militant. Its chief objective was the spiritual and moral regeneration of the church.

The Great Awakening passed, but millenarianism was kept going by a number of happenings. A series of earthquakes in 1755 inspired sermons on the Second Coming and the Judgement Day. The early reversals suffered by the British in their wars with the French over colonies in North America and in conflicts in India intensified apocalyptic forecasting. The fears aroused by the wars subsided once the victory of the British was secure, but where one would have expected millennial hopes to have subsided they were to receive a considerable boost from the American revolution. Congregational ministers were in the vanguard in heralding the coming era of liberty from the British Antichrist and the imminent establishment of the Kingdom of God in the new world. Patriotism and religious sentiment fed one another.

Revolutionary millennialists proclaimed the time when the triumphant American nation would become God's own country, "the principal seat of that new, that peculiar kingdom, which shall be given to the saints of the Most High" (Bloch, 1985, 82). Although American revolutionary millenarianism did not produce an actual blueprint for the new age, it did help to create the new republican order. It encouraged nationalism and dreams of America becoming the leading world power. It gave birth to a version of millennialism which was to contribute to socio-political development, viz. millennialism in the form of enlightenment and progress (Bloch, 93). This liberal dream became a powerful energising force for generations of Americans in years to come.

The Effect of the French Revolution

But it was back in Europe that the greatest momentum in millennial expectation was about to be generated. The cause was the French Revolution (1789). This had the effect of giving awesome reality to the predictions of what life would be like when the vials of God's wrath, forecast in Revelation, were poured out upon the earth. Prophecies of the persecuted and beleaguered Huguenots were read with new interest (Dodge, 1947). The French monarchy and its armies were regarded as the servants of the Beast of Revelation. Roman Catholics, similarly, found in the prophecies of the later Middle Ages the revolution foreshadowed and prayed for the regeneration of the religious orders and the state at large, though the majority of the clergy, aware of the need for spiritual and moral regeneration, began by being less concerned with the reform of the state than the reform of the church (Garrett, 1975, 48-49). The rallying call, "Liberty, Equality and Fraternity", had a distinct millenarian sound for the religiously inclined. The faithful believed that society would become moral, the church regenerated and Christ return and rule for one thousand years.

At the outset events in France were greeted with enthusiasm by many liberal-minded persons in Britain and America. They believed the people of France had thrown off an intolerable tyranny and it ill became anyone in a free country to withhold sympathy or help from those who had suffered so long. A wide spectrum of clergy, from the evangelical David Bogue to the rationalist Joseph Priestley, welcomed the Revolution as the birth of a new age and the sign of the approaching millennium (Bogue and Bennett, 4, 1812, 195-197). Only in the later stages of the conflict, when there seemed to be no end to the reign of terror and when France went to war against the rest of Europe, did opinion change. Instead of Louis XVI being cast in the role of the Antichrist the Revolution itself was now given this role. But at the point when millenarianism might have been thought to have been discredited a new interpretation of the doctrine had seized the imagination of Christians in Europe and in North America. Before we consider this we need to summarise historical millenarianism.

Features of Historic Millenarianism

In reviewing the millenarian movements studied thus far one must say that the outstanding impression conveyed is their optimism about history. Whatever else must be said about them they are not escapist but rooted firmly in this world. The millenarian kingdom is always conceived of as within history. Its terrestrial emphasis is more or less constant in the different movements. Millenarianism is a vision of a just world. Evil and injustice are not absolute and final. Better things are in store for the poor and the oppressed. For all their fantasies, millenarian groups believed that reform was possible and the future could be shaped according to God's will. This is one of the more positive features of historical millenarianism that is not emphasised by Norman Cohn in his classic study of the subject (Worsley 1957).

Millenarianism arises in times of social and political crisis and among groups most affected by change, especially those experiencing unusually harsh suffering, persecution and national disasters. In her study of the subject, Yonina Talmon (1968) regards this as a leading characteristic of millenarianism. She points out that the deprivation is usually accompanied by frustration caused by the inability of people to achieve long-held expectations or by social change leading to new expectations that are left largely unfulfilled. The sense of cultural deprivation and the need for cultural reorientation are sometimes of greater importance than economic deprivation. The appeal of millenarian movements was in no small measure due to their ability to provide their followers with a rationale for their present sufferings and offer them a credible counter culture.

Millenarianism is clearly a response to multiple causes. The views of Norman Cohn that it is a form of mass psychological phenomena and Eric Hobsbawn that the radical movements of the Reformation are essentially movements of social unrest (1965) are thus rightly shown by Worsley and Talmon to be in need of revision. Their studies demonstrate that in millenarianism religious belief, social change, poverty, oppression and political powerlessness all play their part.

Millenarianism is a powerful motivation for action. It demands fundamental change, not amelioration. Its visions authenticate and empower these movements. With God's help nothing is impossible. Opposition and suffering are interpreted as the birth pangs of a new age. Thus millenarianism can be rightly regarded as the harbinger of political action (Talmon, 1968,355-356). Some of its manifestations, such as the Levellers, were remarkably visionary in their ideas of religious freedom, equality and parliamentary reform. Communities of the saints embarked not only on suicidal adventures of armed revolt, but also in significant programmes of reform. Millenarian hope contributed to the American dream of progress and prosperity.

All this should not be taken to mean that millenarianism was embraced by the church at large. This was far from being the case. In the Middle Ages the Catholic Church found itself attacked by millenarian revolutionaries bent on reforming it root and branch. Pope, bishops, clergy and monastic orders were viewed as symbols of the powerful and the privileged and came under the lash of the Latter Day prophets. People were butchered, churches and monasteries were plundered, and bishops found themselves organising armies to quell the marching hordes.

The Protestant churches were similarly hostile to millenarian movements. Where the doctrine was adopted by Protestants it was almost exclusively with small sects, e.g. the Taborites and the Anabaptists. Luther did open the way for the Book of Revelation to be interpreted as a prophecy for the future, but it was only in the seventeenth century that belief in a future millennium came to be widely held and enthusiastically canvassed. It gradually lost its militant features. The excesses of Fifth Monarchists excepted, the eschatology of the rank and file of Puritans and Nonconformists was not a desperate bid to defy the exigencies of history for a future paradise. It was an earnest desire to reform church and state.

Militant millenarianism passed into history with the seventeenth century. New influences were at work. Particularly important was the connection made between the millennium and the rise and spread of foreign missionary work.

III
The Millennium and the Church's Mission

"This gospel of the kingdom will be preached throughout the whole world as a testimony to all nations; and then the end will come" (Matt. 24.14, RSV; cf. Mk.13.10). The connection made here between the evangelisation of the nations and the Second Coming has had a significant influence on millennial thinking, though it was not until the navigators Christopher Columbus and Vasco da Gama broke down the provincialism of Europe and pushed out the horizons of European consciousness that the implications of the command to take the gospel to the nations were grasped by the churches.

The Millennial Kingdom of the Franciscans

Columbus was alive to the possibilities his discoveries held for the missionary task of the church and encouraged his contemporaries to look for the millennial kingdom in the New World. The Observant Franciscans took up the challenge. Like Columbus, they were students of Joachim of Fiore and believed themselves to be in the final great period of history. The New World held a powerful attraction for the twelve Franciscans who arrived in Mexico in 1524. Free of the corruptions and traditions that plagued the old world, the New World presented itself to the Franciscans as a unique opportunity to recover the simplicity and zeal of the church of the apostles. Their resolve to work for the coming of the Kingdom of God was strengthened by the belief that Indians were descendants of the ten lost tribes of Israel.

Genónimo de Mendieta (1525-1604) and the Franciscan missionaries fervently believed that they could create the most authentic form of Christianity the world had ever known and that this would foreshadow the approaching end of the world. Mendieta's writings show him pursuing the hope with total commitment (Phelan, 1970, 69-77). In his struggle to protect Indians from avarice and exploitation, Mendieta battled with crown officials, Spanish settlers, secular clergy and friars no longer committed to a rigorous ascetic ideal. He fought for all his worth against the *repartimento*, which forced Indians to work for Spaniards for a pittance. But although Mendieta was socially concerned he came nowhere near to joining the ranks of the revolutionary millenarianism which had appeared in the first crusade and became such an explosive force in the Protestant movements of the sixteenth century (Phelan, 1970,76-77).

The dream of a millennial kingdom in the New World was ruined for Mendieta by a devastating decline of the Indian population, the effects of Hispanicisation and colonialism and the bureaucratic policies of Philip II. But Mendieta did not give up hope. Like others who have not seen their predictions fulfilled, he revised his apocalyptic timetable. He interpreted the troubles which had befallen the New World and Spain as the Great Tribulation predicted by the Book of Revelation after which the millennium would appear (Phelan, 103-117).

Protestant Missions

It was not until the eighteenth century that world-wide missionary work was undertaken by the Protestant churches. By this time Protestant nations had control of the seas and were influenced by the confluence of a number of happenings. The confidence and spirit of adventure flowing from the Enlightenment in the seventeenth century, the advances in education and science and, more particularly, the Evangelical Revival in England and its counterpart in North America all conjoined with the eschatological urgency of Christ's words to launch the great missionary societies of the eighteenth and nineteenth centuries.

The form which millenarianism took in the world-wide outreach of the Protestant churches and missionary agencies contrasts sharply with the militant forms of Protestant millenarianism we have studied. De Jong, in his study of millennial expectations in the rise of Anglo-American missions from 1640-1810, refers to this type of millenarianism as "mild millennialism". His survey of the pamphlets and sermons which marked the launching of the Baptist Missionary Society (1792), the London Missionary Society (1795) and the Church Missionary Society (1799) shows the extent to which the doctrine of the Last Days lay at the heart of the modern missionary enterprise (de Jong, 1970, 175-198).

William Carey, the father of Protestant missions, challenged the churches: "If the prophecies concerning the increase of Christ's kingdom be true . . . all Christians ought heartily to concur with God in promoting his glorious designs" (1792). Andrew Fuller, friend of Carey and the indefatigable advocate of the Baptist Missionary Society, inspired without doubt by the successes of the mission at Serampore, told an Edinburgh audience in 1799 that the End was at hand. "The last branch of the last of the four beasts is now in its dying agonies. No sooner will it be proclaimed, Babylon is fallen! than the marriage of the Lamb will come" (quoted by de Jong, 181).

David Bogue spoke of the launching of the London Missionary Society as "a history in the epoch of man," the beginning of the spread of the kingdom at home and abroad which would not stop "till the knowledge of God covered the earth as the waters cover the sea" (Lovett, I, 1899, 36). In Bogue's *Discourses on the Millennium* missions are clearly shown to be the agency for realising the latter-day glory of the church. George Burder, another founder of the LMS and the main impulse for the foundation of the Religious Tract Society, made the same connection between missions and the reign of Christ when he said, "Is it not probable that the great Disposer of all is now about, by shaking terribly the nations, to establish that spiritual and extensive kingdom which cannot be shaken?" (Lovett, 21).

The influence of millenarianism in the formation of the CMS was not as pronounced. However, within a decade this society had come to rely on these expectations for its vision and support. Charles Simeon and John Venn, founders of the CMS, held millenarian views, albeit of a moderate kind. At the annual meeting of the CMS in 1811 the familiar note was sounded loud and clear by Melville Horne, "The trumpet of the Millennial Jubilee is at last heard. . . . Serious Christians of all denominations are espousing the cause of missions, and anxious to 'prepare the way of the Lord' " (de Jong, 192).

The same influence was at work in the formation of missionary societies in Scotland. Although overseas missions were rather slower in getting off the ground in Scotland, individuals like David Bogue who played such an important part in the founding of the LMS, were successful in encouraging evangelicals in their desire to engage in overseas mission. The Glasgow Missionary Society and the Edinburgh Missionary Society were formed in 1796 and, as elsewhere, eschatological expectations were an important contributory factor (de Jong, 166-175).

Continental Missions

The expectation of the return of Jesus Christ was a powerful motivating influence for missions in Anabaptist churches in Germany virtually from their beginning. Michael Sattler, writing from his prison in Binsdorf (Württemberg) in 1527, declared "the gospel is proclaimed to all the world – a sign that the day of the Lord cannot be long delayed" (Schäufele, 1966, 81). Melchior Hofmann in the early 1530s regarded the renewed church (the Anabaptists) as the 144,000 of Revelation who would be the bearers of a world-wide wave of missionary activity (Schäufele, 94). The Moravians were similarly influenced by belief in the return of Jesus Christ. Their founder Nikolaus von Zinzendorf (1700-1760) viewed missions as the gathering of the First Fruits before the End. How these Anabaptist and Pietist groups conceived of the evangelisation of the world is difficult to imagine since they expected an early Parousia. Hofmann believed the New Jerusalem would arrive in Strasbourg in 1533.

The Basel Mission, which began in 1815, was strongly influenced by hope of the return of Jesus Christ. At the opening of its headquarters in 1820, Deacon Stockmeyer declared that "a new, apostolic, or in other words, a missionary age was dawning. . . . If the gospel of God's Kingdom is preached over the whole earth there are high hopes of the coming of the Lord in his glory" (Aagaard, 1967, 187). It has to be said that when eschatological expectation reached such a pitch in Württemburg that 1836 was proclaimed as the year of the Lord's return and the beginning of the thousand year reign, all missionary activity came to a halt. Responsibility for this unfortunate state of affairs is attributed to the predictions of Johann Albrecht Bengel (1687-1752): he had foretold that the End would come in 1836. In the event, the influential Christian Friedrich Spittler (1782-1867) helped to revive the mission's eschatological emphasis and its missionary activity was resumed (Aagaard, 203). The Basel Mission grew to become one of the great missionary agencies of Europe.

Similarly, in the Reformed Churches of the continent, eschatology played an important role in launching overseas missionary work. The Paris Missionary Society, founded in 1822, included the Second Coming in what it called "the great supernatural Christian events". Churches were urged to support missionary work overseas and "hasten the happy time when 'all the ends of the earth shall see the salvation of our God' (Isa. 52.10). . . . Let us not delay, the time is short" (*La Société des missions évangéliques,* 1822). Candidates for the Society had to subscribe to its eschatological basis. This created problems in later years when candidates who held liberal theological views began applying to the PMS. In time, this mission, like others, was affected by the upheaval in New Testament scholarship over the eschatological teachings attributed to Jesus and the questions this raised for New Testament eschatology generally. The strict eschatological views of the continental missionary bodies were moderated and emphasis was put more on social involvement (Aagaard, 256; Bosch, 1991, 507-508).

Missions in North America

Across the Atlantic missionary work was gradually becoming the concern of the Protestant churches of New England. Work among the Indians of New England and farther afield had been undertaken intermittently from the time of the Puritan settlers, but, as happened in England, the energising power of the revival movement was needed to secure the support of the churches generally for the missionary enterprise at home and abroad. This was supplied by the Great Awakening from 1760-1780, followed by the Second Great Awakening from 1787-1825 (Chaney, 1976, 101-104; Bosch, 277-283). Sweeping aside the deism and scepticism prevalent among the educated classes, the new movement of the Spirit resulted in home and foreign missionary outreach, abolition of the slave trade and movements of social reform.

Already Jonathan Edwards (1703-1758) had personally set the example. The work begun by his son-in-law, David Brainerd, prior to his early death, encouraged Edwards to become a missionary himself, and he worked for a time among Indians on the Massachusetts border. Edwards was an enthusiastic postmillenarian and spent a good deal of time on the routing of the Antichrist and the coming of the golden age (*Works*, 5). For him the arrival of the millennium would be progressive and gradual; it would make life holier, happier and more prosperous for everyone. His vision drew heavily on Isaiah's prophecy of the lion living in peace with the lamb (11.6) and was strikingly utopian.

Another influential postmillenarian and advocate of missions was Samuel Hopkins (1721-1803), Congregational theologian from Rhode Island (Chaney, 74-75). Hopkins fought against the slave trade and tirelessly encouraged missionary causes throughout his long ministry. In his mind the power and the will for missions lay in the millennial hope. His *Treatise on the Millennium* (1793) interpreted the thousand year reign of Christ as an earthly utopia. He predicted that machines would be invented which would increase production and wellbeing so that people would have leisure to pursue learning of every kind. Universal peace and happiness would fill the earth. At the end of this period Christ would return and reign until his enemies were subjugated and earthly kingdoms "become his own Kingdom". By contrast with the cataclysmic happenings associated with the eschatological age in the Bible, Hopkins's millennium evolves gradually and peacefully. Above all, it is helped on its way by the missionary labours of God's servants.

The foreign missionary movement in the Protestant churches of America began with the formation of the American Board of Commissioners of Foreign Missions (the ABM) in 1810. It owed its beginning to the concern of a number of students converted during the revivals and to the interest of professors at Andover Theological Seminary. Once again, the expectation of the return of Jesus Christ and the establishing of his millennial kingdom were motivating influences. Writings on the End time in England were imported and eagerly studied, but it was the thinking of Edwards and Hopkins which put its stamp on the eschatology of the North American missionary enterprise (de Jong, 222-227). Their postmillennialism was to influence thinking well into the twentieth century.

Continuing Influence of Eschatology on Missions

Eschatology continued to sustain overseas missionary work in the Western world. In England Hudson Taylor, founder of the China Inland Mission (1865), worked tirelessly for the conversion of China's millions in preparation for Christ's return. During the latter half of the nineteenth century numerous interdenominational missions were founded whose basis and inspiration were the coming again of Christ (Capp, 1987, 113; Pocock, 1988, 441-444). D.L. Moody, possessed by the same concern, was a major influence in the formation of the Student Volunteer Movement (1886). Its motto, "The evangelisation of the world in this generation", owed much to the belief that the return of Christ was imminent.

The eschatological imperative in mission exercised a strong influence in all branches of the church well into the twentieth century. The Edinburgh Conference in 1937 (*History and Records*, 150), the International Missionary Council in Willingen in 1952 (Thomas, 1995, 306) and the World Council of Churches Assembly at Evanston in 1954 (*Report to Advisory Group*, 24) all showed the significance of eschatology for the church's mission. The same is true of the International Congress of World Evangelism in Lausanne in 1974 (*Article* 15) and the Wheaton Conference in 1983 (*Message of Wheaton*, 1983).

The influence which eschatology continued to exert on the missionary enterprise owed much to leading missiologist Walter Freytag (1899-1959). Writing at the time of the catastrophe of World War II, Freytag, who was critical of prevailing understandings of God's mission and reign, had no hesitation in affirming belief in God's End-time in bringing in his reign. He declared, "Mission is part of God's *end-time working* . . . the sign of the end time set up by God. . . . Where mission occurs, God shows that his hour is coming closer" (Thomas, 310).

But by this time other influences were at work, which led to belief in the personal return of Jesus Christ ceasing to be an impelling influence in mission in the mainline churches. As we saw, postmillennialism lent itself very easily to a secularised understanding of the millennium (Bloch, 93). It was grafted onto an evolutionary doctrine of progress, and it was inevitable that it should suffer the same fate as belief in progress suffered when the optimistic tenets of the Enlightenment were discredited by the harsh realities of the twentieth century. The goal of world evangelisation remained unrealised. Nor would it help to return to premillennialism and its more realistic view of the world. In the minds of a growing number of Christians the Second Coming of Christ had been delayed too often for it to continue to sustain the missionary movement, except in churches and missionary agencies of a fundamentalist persuasion. By this time churches generally were making increasing use of the historical method of biblical study. The consequences of this approach to the Bible were far-reaching for their understanding of New Testament eschatology. What the New Testament said about the return of Jesus Christ was either questioned or reinterpreted by increasing numbers of students of the New Testament so that it was no longer taken literally. The inspiration for mission was now understood more in terms of the love of God and humanitarian concern.

The Restoration Movement

Surprisingly, postmillennialism has made a fresh appeal in recent times. It has found expression in the Restoration movement in Britain and in the Reconstruction movement in the United States (Pawson, 1995, 256). Highly critical of the mainline churches and denominationalism in general, the Restoration movement believes itself called by God to restore New Testament Christianity. The restored church will be empowered by the Spirit to restore in turn the Kingdom of God. By the zeal of God's servants the Kingdom will grow, like "the stone cut without human hands" of Daniel's vision (2.45), until it crushes all opposition (Walker, 1998, 137-142). In true postmillennial form, the way is thus prepared for the Second Coming of Christ, but inasmuch as most Restorationists believe that evil will still be powerful enough to cause the Great Tribulation of Revelation 7.14 one can hardly describe this as classic postmillennialism. Nonetheless there is no gainsaying the fact that belief in the restored church becoming an unstoppable force in the world in preparation for the Second Coming certainly has a millenarian look about it.

Liberation Theologians

Eschatology was given a new lease of life in the church's mission, albeit in a somewhat different form, by the liberation theologians of Latin America. Understanding the Reign (Kingdom) of God as the definitive eschatological event, these theologians believe that Christianity is essentially a message of hope. The Reign of God is the core of their theology.

> For liberation theology, the ultimate is the Reign of God. This does not mean, of course, that it ignores the resurrection, or that it does not see the clearly eschatological dimension of the resurrection. It is only that, for the purposes of a theology that assigns primacy to the liberation of the poor, it sees the *eschaton* better expressed in terms of the Reign of God (Sobrino, 1993, 352).

The gospels show us Jesus proclaiming the advent of the Reign of God. The hungry, the sick and the ostracised are given hope, while the secure have their world turned upside down. To seek first God's Reign is to seek his righteousness. Since he is righteous he wants righteous dealings on earth. Praxis is thus an essential part of our understanding of the Reign of God and the vocation of the church.

The liberation theologians are emphatic that the Reign of God needs to be historicised and made concrete in personal, social and political ways, though it is more than these. The voices of Christian prophecy are needed if structural injustice and enslaving practices are to be identified, censored and transformed. Christian proclamation contains a "subversive dynamism" (Ellacuria, 1993, 322). Criticising those who say that it is God and God alone who will bring in the Kingdom, Segundo says that such thinking induces in people an irresponsible resignation and passivity, when God is calling them to be his co-workers in bringing in the new order (1977, 147-148).

The utopian or millenarian character of liberation theology is particularly clear in Ignacio Ellacuria's essay *Utopia and Prophecy* (1993, 289-328). He declares that prophecy has the responsibility not only of denunciation but also of providing an alternative model.

> To begin anew a historic order that will transform radically the present one, based on the promotion and liberation of human life, is the prophetic call that can open the way to a new utopia of Christian inspiration (305).

Such an alternative will provide new economic, social, political and cultural orders. In words which have an unmistakable millenarian ring, Ellacuria says that the creation of this new order will mean the creation of a new earth (312-313). The fundamental principle on which the new order should be based remains "that all might have life and have it more abundantly" (John 10.10). Liberation means liberation "from" sin in every shape and form and liberation "for" freedom and justice for all.

Liberation theology has drawn upon the work of German theologians, particularly Johann Baptist Metz and Jürgen Moltmann. Metz challenged theologians to relate their faith to society in a "political theology" which contextualises the eschatological message of the Kingdom of God to conditions of modern society (1969). Moltmann sought to make eschatology central to Christianity by giving a living hope to the future (1967). His emphasis on eschatology is reaffirmed in his book *The Coming of God* (1996) and shown to have particular relevance in millenarianism for today's world. Moltmann surveys the different forms of millenarianism through the ages before addressing the question: is millenarian eschatology necessary? Distinguishing between historical millenarianism and eschatological millenarianism, he says that while the former should be rejected the latter should be affirmed.

> Historical millenarianism is the millenarian interpretation of the present in its political or ecclesiastical aspect, or in the context of universal history. Eschatological millenarianism is an expectation of the future in the eschatological context of the end, and the new creation of the world. Historical millenarianism . . . is a religious theory used to legitimate political or ecclesiastical power, and is exposed to acts of messianic violence and the disappointments of history. Eschatological millenarianism, on the other hand, is a necessary picture of hope in resistance, in suffering and in the exiles of this world. Millenarianism must be firmly incorporated into eschatology. Detached from eschatology, and simply by itself, it leads to the catastrophes of history. But incorporated in eschatology it gives strength to survive and to resist (1996, 192).

Eschatology thus continues to influence the church's mission, though its content has changed. The emphasis has shifted from the expectation of Christ's return to the Kingdom of God which is both present and future. By emphasising God's Reign in the here and now, the liberation theologians attempt to preclude a dualistic understanding of history. They also aim to rule out the passivity so characteristic of some End-time prophecies. Moltmann, or at least the younger Moltmann, differs from the liberation theologians inasmuch as he (from his Lutheran perspective) emphasises the Kingdom as God's gift, but he was later influenced by the liberation theologians to acknowledge that the gratuity of the Kingdom is not opposed to human effort but rather calls for this. At the same time, the Kingdom is future. The so-called "eschatological proviso" safeguards theology from the dangers that Moltmann exposed in *The Coming of God*, when eschatology collapses into history and the millennium is identified with political regimes or ecclesiastical institutions. Because the Kingdom still has to come no present form of life or society can ever be regarded as ultimate. Sobrino succinctly expresses the double character of the Kingdom:

> The theology of liberation knows very well that utopia is that which by definition is never realised in history (*ou topos*) but it also knows that there are *topoi* in history, and that the will of God is better realised in some than in others (383).

The absence of the Second Coming of Christ from liberation theology prompts us to ask whether its eschatology has moved so far in a theocentric direction that Christology has been marginalised. Certainly there is no place in liberation theology for pre- and postmillennialism. Although the Second Coming is not emphasised in liberation theology Jesus Christ is seen as having a crucial place. The Reign of God is centred in Christ, and the life, death and resurrection of Christ is the historical manifestation of God's reign. What God has done and continues to do in and through Jesus Christ he has not done through anyone else.

Summary

The changes in the churches' understanding of the eschatological imperative in mission reviewed in this chapter reflect the difficulty which churches have today in interpreting the eschatology of the New Testament. But even where the hope of the personal and visible return of Jesus Christ to earth or the expectation of a millennial kingdom no longer feature in the understanding of mission in the great majority of the churches today or where eschatology is formulated in terms of the Kingdom of God, it is universally acknowledged that the "eschatological proviso" is essential if the church is not to become wholly preoccupied with the challenges of the here and now. David Bosch, who wrestled with the place of eschatology in mission today, spoke for many when he said that the future must feature in our understanding of mission, adding, "if we turn off the lighthouse of eschatology we can only grope around in darkness and despair" (509). But the question how precisely we should interpret the meaning of the millennium remains a problem. Before we turn our attention to this question we have one further aspect of this introductory section to consider, viz. the imminent End.

IV
The Imminent End

In the nineteenth century a new urgency was introduced into millenarianism. A series of individuals emphasised the imminence of the End and in some cases set a date for it. This development affected the churches in Britain and in the USA and had consequences that are with us still.

Edward Irving

Edward Irving (1792-1834), a Scot, drew great crowds to his fashionable church in London. He emphasised the impending judgements of God on the church, the imminence of Christ's return and his reign on earth. *The Times* published daily extracts from Irving's work (1823). Irving carried the excitement of his message to Scotland in 1828 and he gave early morning lectures at the time of the General Assembly of the Church of Scotland. Gradually, however, the novelty wore off. Irving found himself in trouble with the Church of Scotland over several aspects of his teaching. There was a division within his congregation. Six hundred of his followers went with him into the wilderness, eventually joining the Catholic Apostolic Church. Irving's influence lived on after his early death, and the Irvingite movement started a tradition of millennial expectation that is alive in some circles to this day. In particular, it gave rise to forecasting the actual date of the Second Coming.

John Nelson Darby

Speculation on the date of the Second Coming was intensified by J.N. Darby (1800-1882). He created an impressive time-frame of history which became known as dispensationalism. Dispensational premillenialism is distinguished from the so-called classical premillenialism of the early church fathers inasmuch as it divided history into periods or dispensations.

According to Darby there are seven such dispensations from Noah till the End. The seventh is the millennium. Christ would return before the millennium, but in two stages. In the first stage he would remove the church before the start of the "Great Tribulation" predicted in Revelation. Darby described St Paul's words about believers being "caught up . . . in the clouds to meet the Lord in the air" (1 Thess. 4.17) as the "rapture", which was understood as a secret removal of believers before the traumas of the Great Tribulation. An evil ruler, the Antichrist, would head the most anti-God and socio-economic totalitarianism the world had ever experienced. The Antichrist would be defied by the Jews, however, who in turn would be converted to Christ through their suffering. Finally, in what is the second stage of the End time, at the point when the Antichrist forces are about to annihilate the remaining believing Jews, Christ would come in power with his saints and destroy the Antichrist and his minions. Thereafter he would establish his Kingdom over the whole world. It would endure for one thousand years. This is the Kingdom Christ initially offered the Jews at his incarnation. When they rejected it, God withdrew it and postponed it till the millennium. Jesus' teaching on the Kingdom, particularly the Sermon on the Mount, is primarily applicable to the millennial era.

This "dispensational" brand of premillennialism was widely popularised in the *Scofield Reference Bible*, first published in 1909. This Bible had an enormous influence. Its extensive notes and comments on the Second Coming contributed to the place the subject holds in modern fundamentalism (Sandeen, 1970, 62-64).

Darby's dispensationalism resulted in a very negative view of the church and the world. The church belonged to the dispensation that had failed. God's method is not to restore it but to replace it. Movements for the reform of the church and the world, like the world-wide missionary enterprise, are thus misguided. "Instead of permitting ourselves to hope for a continued progress of good, we must expect a progress of evil" (*Collected Works* I, 471). The pessimism in Darby's view of things is in sharp contrast to the optimism of the millenarian movements we studied in the previous chapter. We shall find it reappearing.

William Miller

William Miller (1782-1849) was a Massachusetts farmer turned prophet who exercised considerable influence in America (Nichol, 1945). In 1831 when invited to speak at a small church in a nearby town Miller preached on Daniel. His message was so warmly received and caused such alarm that he was prevailed upon to begin teaching on the Second Coming. He published his first book, *Evidences from Scripture and History of the Second Coming of Christ About the Year 1843*.

It was not Miller's intention to set up in opposition to the churches, but church leaders grew increasingly worried as the Millerites interpreted the scriptures literally and became obsessed with the imminent return of Christ. Miller abandoned his anti-slavery campaigning to concentrate on his advent teaching. His separation from the churches became inevitable. When 1843 arrived without the End his followers dealt with their disappointment by standing together against the rest of the world. Calling themselves the Adventists, they became a denomination of their own and set a new date for the Second Coming: 22 October 1844. When the revised date passed without incident those who had disposed of their homes and settled their worldly affairs in expectation of the millennium were devastated. The Millerites became the object of ridicule and scorn. Some returned to their former churches; others joined the Shakers, while others abandoned religion altogether. But a significant number remained loyal to the movement and subsequently increased in numbers. Today they are known as the Seventh Day Adventists (St. Clair, 1992, 317).

It was not only the mistake of setting a date for the End that harmed millenarianism. Another contributory factor was its negative view of society. Millerism made a point of cataloguing the evils of society and natural disasters as evidence of the approaching end of the world. Its tragic view of history owed something to the social and political events of the time. The depression of 1831 and its aftermath and the difficulties encountered by the anti-slavery and temperance movements took their toll. Social movements came to be regarded as a waste of time by people who believed that God would put right the problems of the world at a single stroke. Millenarianism now began to look decidedly other-worldly and socially irresponsible (Barkum, 1986, 494).

Millenarianism did eventually recover from the Millerite debacle in the conservative churches. It was helped to a great extent by the dispensational interpretation of C.I. Scofield (and his famous Bible) and D.L. Moody. On the wider church scene, the doctrine, like the eschatology of the New Testament in general, was re-examined and reinterpreted as a result of the growing use of the historical critical approach to the Bible. Belief in Christ's return on the clouds was superseded by the idea of God's Kingdom in this world, which would be brought in by the faithful work of missionaries abroad and the creation of an egalitarian society on the home front. By 1917 Walter Rauschenbusch, leading exponent of the now popular social gospel, was optimistically declaring that the Kingdom of God was "itself the social gospel" (Hopkins, 1940, 20).

The Jehovah's Witnesses

In the aftermath of the non-fulfilment of William Miller's predictions various small Adventist groups reacted by setting new dates for the Second Coming. One of these groups attracted an enthusiastic young man named Charles Taze Russell (1852-1916). Although Russell believed that Miller had got his dates wrong, he regarded Miller's attempt to discern the times prior to the end of the world as justifiable (1926, 86). Russell's fascination with the End, the Second Coming of Christ, Armageddon and the millennium was later to influence strongly, the Jehovah's Witnesses, the movement that followed him (Crompton, 1996). Russell believed Christ was choosing a church of 144,000 (Rev. 7.4; 14.1), whose resurrection would be completed in 1881. He went on to reject the doctrine of the Trinity and broke farther away from his former Adventist friends. He finally concluded that Christ would visibly return to earth to establish his millennium kingdom in 1914. A new date was set for the End by Russell's successor, Judge Joseph Franklin Rutherford. He predicted 1926. Many people gave up their businesses and jobs and sold their homes, believing they were about to enter an earthly paradise (Penton, 1985, 58). Thousands left the movement in disillusionment. In 1931 the movement became known as Jehovah's Witnesses.

The Kingdom of God, according to the Jehovah's Witnesses, is in heaven. By a remarkable piece of chronology the Kingdom was believed to have been established in 1914 (*Revelation: its Grand Climax at Hand*, 1988, 104-106). From this point in time Christ was said to rule along with the 144,000 or more correctly those of them who have reached heaven. In addition, the church includes many others, the "great crowd" (Rev. 7.9) or the "other sheep" (John 10.16), who will live for ever in Paradise restored on earth, provided they remain faithful to Jehovah. In the meantime life in this world is marked by war, natural disasters, epidemics and increasing lawlessness and false prophets. It is in the grip of Satan. It is in fact irredeemable. "Bringing an end to this system of things . . . is the only way to rid the world of evil and make room for peace and righteousness to flourish (*The Good News of the Kingdom*. 1954, 25). Only when God's Kingdom takes the place of the Satanically controlled kingdoms of the earth will there be peace and well-being. Before that happens there will be a fight to the finish between the godless nations and Christ and his army (Rev. 19.11-21). This is the battle of Armageddon described in Revelation 16.12-16 (Crompton, 76-94).

According to the Jehovah's Witnesses Armageddon is a war that will be fought not locally but globally. It will be the most devastating war in human history. All the wicked of the world and every evil institution will be destroyed. The only way to survive Armageddon is to join the Jehovah's Witnesses.

In the meantime the millennial rule of Christ and the saints is taking place in heaven. It is a literal period of one thousand years. The new earth or more correctly the renewed earth has to wait until the end of the millennium. "By the end of the Thousand Year Reign, all earth will have come to resemble the original Eden. It will be a veritable paradise" (*Revelation: Its Grand Climax at Hand*, 291). To this restored world the resplendent New Jerusalem will descend and channel God's blessings to the whole universe (310).

Like apocalyptic movements generally, the Jehovah's Witnesses have had their problems over dates. However, in spite of miscalculations and disappointments they resolutely believe that this Satanically controlled world order is coming to an end and the new world order is a certainty.

Recent End-Time Predictions

Recent years have seen a number of attempts to date the End and even to precipitate it. The response given to Hal Lindsey's books, *The Late Great Planet Earth* in 1970 and *The 1980s: Countdown to Armageddon* in 1981, showed how predictions of the End can tap into subconscious fears and generate much interest.

Lindsey claimed to have established the datum line from which calculations concerning the End should proceed. This was the setting up of the state of Israel in 1948. Previous attempts to interpret contemporary events had failed because the datum line was not known. The return of the Jews to Palestine, repeatedly predicted in Old Testament prophecy, pointed to the "seven year count-down" for the events leading to the End. The powerful enemy from the north described in Ezekiel 38-39, who would "launch an attack on them which sets off the last war of the world", was Russia. Ignoring the way in which others had made fools of themselves by predicting the date of the End, Lindsey declared that the End would come in "this generation" (Matt. 24.34). He did however cover himself to some extent by defining a generation as "something like forty years" (*1970, 43*).

When the Soviet Union collapsed Lindsey wrote a new book, *Planet Earth – 2000 AD: Will Mankind Survive?* (1994), in which he changed his apocalyptic timetable. He maintained that although Russia was no longer a super-power it remained a threat because of its nuclear arsenal and an alliance it would form with Iran, the leader of Israel's dangerous new enemy: Islam. Iran, the dominant member of the alliance, would force Russia into war with Israel (169-202).

This pessimistic view of history is a familiar one. Lindsey simply updated it. The world is threatened not only by Communism but by war, corruption and the growth in hedonism, crime, drugs, violence and interest in the occult. Technological achievement loses its appeal because of the engulfing moral decay. To make matters worse, the church, which should be God's agent of salvation, has itself been deceived and is leading people astray by its apostasy.

In playing upon the fears of people Lindsey was following the example of Doomsday prophets before him. What marked him off from them is the fact that he did not actively encourage his readers to withdraw from public life. Jerry Falwell, Pat Robertson and others of the New Christian Right embraced adventist teaching and political activism to the puzzlement of commentators. These Christians did not see themselves as passive spectators resigned to the End but as participants in the cosmic drama, fighting on God's side for the cause of righteousness (O'Leary, 1994, 172-179). However, unlike more recent millenarian movements, there was no hint of the possible use of arms to hasten the End.

In South Korea the numerous strongly fundamentalist Protestant churches have been fertile ground for the growth of apocalyptic movements, although it would be simplistic to attribute these movements to purely religious origins (Thompson, 1997, 238-245). Incredible trouble was caused when Lee Jang Rim, leader of the Mission for the Coming Days, predicted that Jesus Christ would return at midnight on 28 October 1992. In the widespread disruption that followed, thousands of Rim's followers quit their jobs, sold their homes, divorced their spouses and deserted the armed forces. The entire nation was so overtaken by anxiety and panic that large numbers of riot police had to be deployed to deal with the expected trouble. The debacle caused considerable humiliation and distress among evangelicals generally. It did not, however, dampen the Parousia hope (Chandler, 1993, 261-262).

Dr. David Yonggi Cho, pastor of South Korea's huge Yoidoo Full Gospel Church, is careful not to suffer the fate of the much-derided Lee Jang Rim by setting a date for the return of Christ, but he is in no doubt that it will happen before long. He firmly believes that the Antichrist has begun his work. When the Great Tribulation starts the church will be taken up into heaven. There will be war and devastation caused by a new American or Russian nuclear weapon called a "space bus", but that is only a prelude to the appalling terrors awaiting the world at Armageddon. A Chinese army of 200 million soldiers will engage with the army of the Antichrist. Corpses will pile up like mountains. Then Christ will come. What remains of the two armies will join to fight him, but he will be victorious. With evil out of the way the millennium will appear. The earth will be populated with saints "who neither commit sin nor are affected by illness" (Thompson, 234).

We enter a more sinister world with the Branch Davidians of Waco. At its outset the community at Mount Carmel outside Waco did not differ greatly from other groups obsessed with the end of the world. But when David Koresh (previously Vernon Howell) took over leadership in 1988 its character changed ominously. Using his remarkable knowledge of the Bible, Koresh heightened the group's apocalyptic awareness. He believed that the "seven seals" of the Book of Revelation were in process of being broken open and he prepared for the coming battle between good and evil by rebuilding Mount Carmel as an armed camp.

Debate raged in and out of court over the question who fired the first shot and who it was who started the fire that destroyed the compound and its inhabitants following the siege by the federal officers in February 1993, but certain things are not in dispute. The armed attack on the community was a carbon copy of the sect's apocalyptic view of the End. Damian Thompson's study of the sect leaves him in no doubt that "The Davidians' millenarian beliefs are the most important single factor in the drama of Waco" (296).

In Japan violent millenarianism manifested itself in the cult named Aum Shinrikyo, responsible for the sarin nerve-gas attack in the Tokyo underground on 20 March 1995. In the weeks after the underground attack police who raided the headquarters and other places seized a hoard of 200 tonnes of lethal chemicals, firearm components, great quantities of laboratory equipment, computers, gold, and $8.4 million in cash. Other evidence found suggested that the cult had been conducting research into nuclear, biological and laser weapons (Thompson 250-251).

Aum Shinrikyo (Search for Supreme Truth) was founded by a guru who called himself Shoko Asahara. He published an interpretation of the Book of Revelation (1989) in which he made predictions about the numbers that would die at Armageddon. But any hopes he entertained of saving part of the world's population seemed to have been abandoned and the sect saw itself increasingly as set over against an evil world. In 1995 Aum brought out a book called *A Doom is Nearing the Land of the Rising Sun*. The introduction claims that at the beginning of 1995 Asahara had predicted a huge earthquake in the Kobe region and darkly hints that it was caused by secret technology from the USA. It says that this is a warning. Thompson thinks that the warning, which was issued only a short time before the sarin attack in the underground, "cannot be dismissed as typical Aum hyperbole. In the transcripts of discussions between Asahara and his disciples, most of whom describe themselves as scientists, there is much talk of the uses and effects of chemical and biological weapons, including sarin" (Thompson, 265). Mystery surrounds the attack in the underground. Whether it was diversionary or a trial run for mass genocide remains unclear. But enough is known about Aum Shinrikyo to classify it as a violent millennial cult (Thompson 265).

The New Age Movement

The New Age Movement has a strong utopian or millenarian character. It is, in the words of its followers, "an emerging world view" (Hanegraaff, 1996, 113-119). In the astrological terminology frequently used by New Age, the sun is setting on the old mechanistic and rationalistic age of Pisces and the new spiritual age of Aquarius is dawning. The old age has been judged and found wanting. It produced the nuclear horror, the environmental crisis, and is responsible for much of what threatens life today. It is passing, along with the failed religions of the world. The New Age of Aquarius is on its way.

How the new order of things arrives is variously understood by different New Age thinkers. In some cases it is cataclysmic. In others it is conceived of as a gradual evolution. The apocalyptic thinking of the New Age owes a great deal to Edgar Cayce (1877-1945). Although Cayce lived well before the emergence of the New Age movement he has had a considerable influence on it. He predicted momentous "earth changes" would happen between 1958 and 1998. The earth's gravity poles would shift and earthquakes and floods cause havoc. Large areas of the coasts of America would disappear under the sea. The world's climate would change, with the result that the ice age would return to Europe. Out of the chaos Atlantis would rise from the sea. It is a vision that has appealed to many New Age writers (Hanegraaff, 310, 353).

Some New Age predictions use ideas from the New Testament, like the Second Coming of Christ, the Antichrist and the battle of Armageddon. Already the "Christ presence (Christ life, Christ energy, etc.) has become fully available, and this is what is meant by the term 'Second Coming' " (Hanegraaff, 334). George Trevelyan speaks of a "Second Coming" when he heralds "a New Birth on a planetary and cosmic scale" (1979, 22). Hanegraaff points out:

> Although New Age believers may talk about the 'second coming of the Christ', they do not necessarily believe that this event will involve the appearance of a visible person. Some of them do . . . but others expect the second coming to be a purely spiritual event which will be felt and experienced within, rather than seen with physical eyes (101).

New Age expectations concerning the future reached a high point on 16

August 1987, when large numbers of New Agers assembled at "power centres" around the world to celebrate the "Harmonic Convergence". But like other End-time watchers they had to find ways of explaining the fact that their hopes were dashed.

The age of Aquarius has many of the utopian features which we have come across in our study of millennial movements, along with the belief that the new age will bless humanity with new levels of consciousness. But whereas the movements we have considered see the millennium as part of the linear process of time which leads to a final future, New Age millennialism is part of an astronomical cycle, which is interpreted astrologically. What the recurring astronomical cycles hold in store for the future and whether something greater lies beyond the millennium does not appear to be discussed, but it is a logical question. Hanegraaff acknowledges that "overall theories about the meaning and end of history do exist, but their relation – if any – to the theory of astrological cycles is far from clear. From a theoretical perspective, this situation creates interesting problems which might well turn the millenarianism debate into new directions" (102). New Ageism is constantly mutating, and the age of Aquarius may not be the end of the story. But for New Agers Aquarius seems to be enough to be getting on with, at least for the present.

Features of Present-Day End-Time Predictions

This chapter serves to qualify the findings of earlier chapters. The contrast between the world-denying nature of most of the predictions examined in this chapter and the world-affirming movements of the Middle Ages, and the sixteenth and seventeenth centuries, could scarcely be greater. Here the world is viewed as so hopelessly evil that it must be replaced by a new order. Millenarianism thus becomes increasingly apocalyptic and activistic. As the problems of the world grow in size and complexity millenarian groups become impatient with the attempts of politicians, economists and scientists to bring about changes. In their frustration they are often no longer prepared to wait passively for evil to be destroyed and the new age to be ushered in; they will make it happen. The modern representations of this radical outlook are not the first to believe themselves to be God's chosen instruments in bringing in the new world. Movements like the Taborites also believed this. The differences with today's movements is that they have at their disposal weapons of mass destruction, which give them the potential to wreak havoc out of all proportion to their size or importance (Hubback, 1996).

The widely held view that millennialism is the religion of the socially disadvantaged and oppressed classes needs qualification. The people who were influenced by Edward Irving, Hal Lindsey or the members of the Waco or Aum Shinrikyo sects were not victims of social deprivation like those who swelled the ranks of the millennial movements of earlier times. Many adherents of present day millenarianism are relatively affluent, well read and highly qualified professionals. This means that when people who do not suffer economically and socially read the Book of Revelation and the sufferings it forecasts for the faithful they do so by means of a rhetorically induced perception (O'Leary, 11). They are suffering, but their sufferings are not caused by hostile totalitarian leaders but by principalities and powers that influence their culture and threaten their beliefs.

The tension between the present and the future, between life as it is lived in this world and what one may look forward to, or in New Testament terms, between what believers now experience and what they still have to wait for, is intensified in recent forms of millennialism. Threats of an unprecedented nature, like the escalating world population, growth in drug trafficking, international terrorism, militant fundamentalist movements, all serve to fuel apocalyptic speculation. The dating of the End gives these movements focus and strength, but it also proves to be their undoing.

The question how such movements have the capacity to survive the embarrassment and ignominy caused by the non-fulfilment of their predictions intrigues observers. The answer is to be found partly in the psychological mechanism known as cognitive dissonance. Those who are responsible for making the predictions are unable to accept that they were wrong and protect themselves from anguish and ignominy by rationalising the predictions shown to be untrue so that they appear after all to be true (Festinger, 1962). They may have got the date wrong but they do not believe themselves mistaken in regard to their interpretation of the times. But these movements also continue to make their appeal because they are seen to address fundamental human concerns. It is important to recognise that for all their paranoia they are articulating the anxieties of many moderns in regard to an uncertain world and an uncertain future.

The use made of the Book of Revelation in the End-time prophecies examined in this chapter calls for comment. Before we begin our study of Revelation it is necessary to say something about the way in which Revelation is used by the sects in question. This consists in searching the Bible for parallels to contemporary events that endanger life or threaten to undermine faith in God. Great play is made of the wars and rumours of wars, the earthquakes, famines and other sufferings predicted by Jesus (Mark 13.7-8 and parallels) and the build-up of evil before the final battle of good and evil described in Revelation as Armageddon (Rev. 16.12-16). No attention is paid to principles of biblical scholarship now widely practised in interpreting the Bible. Thus Revelation is not approached as primarily a message for its own time and particular parts of it are not viewed in the light of the whole of the book. Instead, bits of Revelation are taken out of context and joined with predictions from the gospels and epistles in an attempt to present a coherent picture of the End. No attention is paid to the differences of literary genre in the various books of the Bible.

In the following chapters we shall attempt to understand the circumstances in which the Book of Revelation was written before we consider what it has to say about the millennium.

PART TWO

THE BOOK OF REVELATION

V

Understanding the Book of Revelation

A very Different Kind of Book

John calls his book a "revelation of Jesus Christ", which, he tells us, God gave him for the churches (1.1). The word "revelation", from the Greek word *apokalupsis*, links the book with the genre of ancient Jewish literature known nowadays as apocalyptic. The term apocalyptic is used in different senses. Its more restricted sense refers to a particular literary genre, while its wider sense refers to thinking and writing about the end of the present world order, conceived of in some cases as the end of the world and in other cases as a preparation for the new age. The term apocalyptic is also used for experiences so catastrophic and traumatic or to movements so pre-occupied with cosmic disaster that they can be described as End-time. Specialists in apocalyptic today use a threefold classification: "apocalypses" for literary works, "apocalyptic eschatology" for world views, and "apocalypticism" for socio-religious thought-forms or movements. The first and second of these categories are particularly useful for our understanding of Revelation. But essential as a knowledge of the apocalyptic genre is for reading Revelation an appreciation of what John owes to Christian trad-itions is paramount.

It is important to recognise that misunderstanding has often arisen over the dramatic terms in which the End is described. This has frequently led students of apocalyptic to suppose that what is meant is the end of the physical world and the coming of a new age which belongs to the eternal world. This introduces a dualism that owes more to Greek thought than to the Hebrew prophets and their successors in the intertestamental period. In their thinking, the age to come is always established on earth. Beyond the catastrophe resulting from God's judgements history will continue. It is against this background that we can begin to understand John's determin-ation to see the earth rid of the Beast and the throne of God and the Lamb set up upon earth. It also helps us understand that when John pictures the End in terms of a cosmic collapse, he does not mean the end of the world but the end of the idolatrous imperial power.

Apocalyptic was long viewed with suspicion by scholars because of its strange imagery and misuse by fanatics. Consequently the Book of Revelation has been neglected by students of the Bible. Today apocalyptic is less of a problem. Moderns are only too well aware of the threats to the world from pollution, destruction of natural resources, over-population, ethnic wars and weapons of mass destruction in the hands of terrorists or rogue nations. For us the end of life on earth is not an unthinkable possibility.

John's predictions of disaster may not be fulfilled in the ways he expected, but his basic perceptions are not easily challenged. But perhaps it is John's critique of the effects of the ideology of the Roman Empire and the alternative he offers which have done most to make Revelation more popular in theological circles today. The enduring importance of apocalyptic is its power to confront the dominant culture and offer the faithful an alternative to the world of present experience. It addresses perennial human needs and has an indispensable role to play in the modern world.

It cannot be too strongly emphasised that the key to understanding apocalyptic is the recognition that this literary genre is a product of the imagination. No end of confusion and trouble has been caused by the failure to recognise that this literature should not be taken literally. Apocalyptic deals in metaphor, parable and myth. Interpretation requires not only a sympathy for this type of writing and a knowledge of the Old Testament, in particular the books of Daniel and Ezekiel, but also a grasp of John's purpose in writing his book. As often as not, John provides his readers with clues that help in interpreting his imagery.

John's over-riding concern is to address a crisis of faith. The Roman Empire reigned supreme, deceiving its citizens by its power, stability, and the peace and prosperity which many of them enjoyed. Those who questioned the regime or refused to take part in the imperial cult risked serious trouble. John is honest enough to acknowledge that some of his church members had been led astray by the benefits of Roman rule and had compromised themselves by their involvement, directly or indirectly, in the Emperor's cult. Consequently, John's primary task is to challenge the reigning ideology. What he does is to counter the threat posed to Christian faith by presenting a vision of an alternative symbolic universe (Hanson, 1979, 434). The understanding of reality he offers the churches is designed to help them see that the power structures of their world are not what they appear to be. They are illusory and temporal. In the new symbolic universe "the kingdom of the world has become the kingdom of our Lord and of his Messiah and he will reign for ever and ever" (11.15). It is his hope that his readers by appropriating this vision will be motivated and empowered to witness to the gospel in a hostile environment.

In order to get a perspective on what is happening on earth, John is taken up into heaven. He then returns to earth to interpret what is happening. The vision keeps alternating between earth and heaven. In other words, the Book of Revelation is not a flight into a fantasy world. It is revelation for living here and now.

Who Wrote it?

John gives us his name (1.1; cf. 1.4, 9). The first Christian writer to comment on the authorship of Revelation is Justin Martyr. Writing about AD160, he describes John as one of "the apostles of Christ" (*Dialogue with Trypho* 8.1). Irenaeus (*c.* AD180) is the earliest known writer to say that Revelation, the Fourth Gospel and the Johannine epistles were all written by John the disciple of Jesus (*Against Heresies* 3.11.1-3; 4.20.11). However, the case for believing that Revelation was written by one of the twelve apostles is not strong, even if there is a possibility that John the apostle moved to Asia Minor. The way John describes himself does not suggest that he was an apostle (1.1,9a). The differences in language, style and thought are so great that it is unlikely that Revelation and the Fourth Gospel were written by the same person.

The only status John claims for himself is implied in the description of the book as a prophecy (1.3; 22.7, 9,18-19; cf. 10.11). In fact, this is a key to understanding his book. Like the classical prophets of Israel, John brings the word of God to bear upon the life of the people. He pronounces God's judgement upon a corrupt order and in God's name offers a better order. John communicates to us with conviction because he himself was person-ally affected by the crisis that had overtaken the Empire and the churches. He tells us that he had been banished to the island of Patmos (1.9). This lays the groundwork for what follows.

John's extensive use of the Old Testament and knowledge of the temple of Jerusalem suggest that he was a Jewish Christian. At the same time his intimate knowledge of the topography of western Asia Minor make it likely that he resided there, whilst his detailed description of the merchandise which flowed into Rome makes us wonder whether he did not have a firsthand acquaintance with the mercantile life of the Empire. R.J. Bauckham believes that John's knowledge of the social and economic life of the Empire is "one of the best pieces of evidence for John's engagement with the real-ities of Roman power as experienced by his contemporaries" (1993a, 351).

Why was it written, and when?

There is much about suffering in Revelation (1.9; 2.9-10,13; 3.10; 6.9; 7.13-14; 11.7-8; 12.1-17; 13.7; 16.6; 17.6; 18.24; 19.2) and the vindication of those who lay down their lives in martyrdom (2.7, 11, 17, 26-28; 3.5,12,21; 6.9-11; 7.14; 12.11; 13.7; 15.2; 20.4). However, we should not assume that this means that a wide-scale persecution had broken out in Western Asia Minor. It is true that we hear of the execution of Antipas in 2.13, but this seems to have been an exception. While John may have had in mind the martyrs who died in Nero's attack on the Christians in Rome in 6.9-10, other references to suffering and martyrdom (e.g., 7.13-14; 15.2; 16.6; 17.6) are likely to be understood as predictions, intended to prepare the church for what was still to come.

Readers of Revelation have often found a clue to its date by decoding the seven-headed Beast of chapter 17 as a series of emperors, of whom five have fallen. There is a problem, however: do we start counting from Julius Caesar (45-44BC), Augustus (27BC-AD14) or Tiberius (AD14-37)? And should the three emperors who had only very brief reigns be included (Galba, Otho, Vitellius)? If we start with Augustus and omit the three short reigns we arrive at Domitian (AD81-96). A date for Revelation in Domitian's reign has been widely accepted on the grounds that early Christian writers from Mileto of Sardis onward (mid-second century) regarded Domitian as the next notorious persecutor after Nero. Eusebius (c.180) also lends his weight to the view that Revelation came from the latter part of Domitian's reign and he was followed by many others. But there is no evidence in contemporary writings of a widespread action against Christians in Western Asia Minor in the first century. If there had been such persecution it would surely have been cited in the letter which Pliny, governor of Bithynia, sent to Emperor Trajan in AD112 (*Ep.* 10.96) or in his copy of Trajan's reply (10.97). Pliny was asking for advice on the trial of Christians; if there had been a precedent it would have been quoted. Similarly, the letters of Ignatius say nothing about martyrs. This is strange since some of the churches to whom Ignatius wrote are churches addressed by John (Ephesus, Smyrna, Philadelphia). Furthermore, in recent scholarship doubt has been thrown on the negative reputation of Domitian as a persecutor of the church (Thompson, 1990, 95-115). When all this is taken into consideration the conclusion seems inescapable: no widespread action had been taken against Christians in western Asia Minor in the first century.

A case for a date which connects Revelation with a verifiable persecution was made out by J.A.T. Robinson (1976, 220-252). He argues that Revelation comes from the traumatic years following the vicious attack on Christians in Rome by Nero in AD64 and the events in Palestine leading up to the destruction of Jerusalem in 70. In 66 Vespasian began putting down the Jewish rebellion in Galilee. In June 68, following revolts in Gaul and Spain, Nero was replaced by Galba and killed himself. Early in 69 Galba was killed and Otho became emperor, only to be routed three months later by Vitellius, when Otho took his life. Before 69 was out Vitellius in turn was attacked and put to death by Vespasian. He established himself with the help of his sons Titus and Domitian. Titus destroyed Jerusalem in 70 and later Masada, after the mass suicide of Jews.

These traumatic events may very well have appeared to Christians as signs of the End. It is not difficult to see how Revelation 11.1-13 could have been based on the siege of Jerusalem or how the description of "Babylon" (Rome), torn by civil war (17.12-17) and destroyed by fire (17.16; 18.8-9), could have been influenced by what happened in 64 and 68-69. The Beast whose mortal wound was healed very likely refers to the rumour that Nero had not in fact died but would return with armies from the East.

The earlier dating of Revelation has commended itself to a number of scholars. Others, however, still connect the book with the persecution it is believed that Domitian initiated in about AD95. I myself believe that it was written in the early nineties. John's lifetime had been marked by a series of grim events: the barbarity of Nero's attack on the Christians of Rome; the devastating outcome of the four-year Jewish war which ended in AD70 with Jerusalem in total ruin; the suicide of Nero and the chaos that ensued, as four claimants battled for the imperial throne; and the volcanic eruption of Vesuvius which obliterated seaside towns and spread a pall of darkness far beyond the Bay of Naples. In Asia Minor local attacks were directed at the churches by the authorities. Antipas had been executed; John himself was incarcerated on Patmos. No doubt all this set alarm bells ringing for John. But there were further reasons why John felt impelled to write. He had looked long and hard at the way Rome ruled the world and was concerned at the power of the imperial ideology and its capacity to beguile and deceive its citizens, and he delivered a thoroughgoing criticism of the system and presented God's alternative.

John's chief concern is to tell the world the truth about the regime of Rome and to point it to the true ruler: God Almighty and the Lamb. In doing so he exposed himself and others to the fury of Rome. What we have to note is that the suffering described in Revelation results from witnessing to what the word of God has to say about the world.

> It is a serious mistake to suppose that Revelation opposes the Roman Empire solely because of its persecution of Christians. Rather Revelation advances a thorough-going prophetic critique of the system of Roman power. It is a critique which makes Revelation the most powerful piece of political resistance literature from the period of the early Empire. It is not simply because Rome persecutes Christians that Christians must oppose Rome. Rather it is because Christians must dissociate themselves from the evil of the Roman system that they are likely to suffer persecution (Bauckham, 1993b, 38).

But as we read Revelation it soon becomes clear that John's trenchant criticism of the imperial system is also a criticism of all who are deceived by it – including the churches. The letters to these churches in chapters two and three indicate the extent to which their witness was being harmed by compromise and complicity with the system. How seriously John viewed this and how urgently he saw the need to deal with it is clear from the fact that it is placed at the beginning of his book. Only a renewed church could hope to survive the coming ordeal.

John's critique of the political and economic regime and his appeal to the churches to reform so that they will be better able to stand up to the blandishments of the Empire and witness to the truth of the gospel are the twin themes that run throughout the book. They are indispensable to our understanding of the vision of the millennial kingdom towards the end of the book.

How was it written?

How John wrote his book has puzzled readers from the earliest times. The structure of the book is a problem. It has numerous parallel passages and a number of breaks in the narrative. The book has two major sections. The first section (1.9-3.22) describes John's commission to write to the seven churches. The second and much longer section contains the visions. It is when we look more closely at the second section that things become less clear. Uncertainties begin as soon as the Lamb starts opening the seals of the scroll. The seven seals (6.1-17 and 8.1) are followed by seven trumpets (8.6-11.15) and these by seven bowls of plagues (15.1-16.21). These successive judgements look as if they follow one another chronologically. The judgements grow in intensity: the seals affect a quarter of the population (6.8), the trumpets a third (9.18) and the bowls affect all (16.20). But on closer examination one gets the impression that each cycle of seven finishes in such a way that it has every appearance of being the End (6.12-17; 11.14-15; 16.17-21). This has led numerous scholars to explain the structure of the book in terms of recapitulation. Recapitulation is the repetition of the same basic idea under a series of different images. It is used for rhetorical effect (Giblin, 1994).

The recapitulation theory, which goes back as far as Victorinus of Pettau (*c*.275-300), was questioned when source criticism suggested that the repetitions can be explained on the ground that Revelation was composed by the compilation of various sources. In recent times when the unity of Revelation has been re-emphasised the recapitulation theory has been revived in its original or modified form (White, 1989). Whatever may be said for recapitulation, it is clear that John has a particular fondness for conveying the one and the same reality under different images and viewing it in different ways. Aune, who himself questions the recapitulation theory, writes:

> That does not mean, however, that many of the constituent visions and traditions used as sources by the author could not have referred to essentially the same eschatological events from different perspectives and used variegated imagery (1997, xciii).

How to Interpret Revelation?

Revelation has been interpreted in a variety of ways. Some scholars argue that the book relates directly to events at the time of writing or soon thereafter. There is much to be said for this view. John himself says that he is writing about "what must soon take place" (1.1). Throughout his writing he is challenging and encouraging his hard-pressed churches. If his words were to have any meaning for the churches then they had to be seen as addressing their immediate concerns. But the remarkable way in which Revelation has been found to have a message for later generations means that it cannot be said to relate exclusively to its historical setting.

The second interpretation treats the book as a veiled record of the whole of human history, from the time of Jesus Christ to the end of the world. This view helps to make the message relevant to the contemporary world, but it tends to lose contact with the historical setting of Revelation. Problems arise, moreover, when people believe themselves to be living in the last times and attempt to interpret contemporary movements as presaging the millennium.

The third interpretation sees Revelation as referring directly to the final period of history, culminating in the build-up of evil, the return of Jesus Christ and the replacement of the present evil world by a new order. This futuristic interpretation ignores John's declared intention of writing about happenings of his own time. It negates his very obvious pastoral concern to help his churches witness to Jesus Christ during a very difficult period.

The fourth way of interpreting Revelation regards the book as containing timeless principles. This says that John is using traditional symbols to depict the ever-present struggle between God and those who attempt to usurp his rule and the ultimate victory of God and justice over evil. Thus the millennium is understood as God's vindication of those who are unjustly treated whenever or wherever they appear. This is a useful way of interpreting Revelation, but it can hardly be said to do justice to the urgency with which John wrote.

The number and variety of interpretations is bewildering, but they do make two things clear. First, they show that attention should be paid to the historical context of the book. Second, Revelation has a religious message that extends far beyond its historical context. Reading Revelation from within their own contexts today people discover meanings for themselves as its message taps into their concerns.

This leads us into what is another matter of debate among biblical scholars, viz. the relative importance of the historical context and intention of the author of the text *vis-à-vis* what the reader sees in the text. I myself regard the task of attempting to establish the intention of the author to be indispensable to interpreting the text. The questions "for whom was it written?" "when?" and "why?" cannot be dismissed. At the same time, I am well aware that interpreting a text depends not simply upon knowing the intention of the author but also the perspective from which the reader approaches the text and his or her agenda in today's world.

What has the Book of Revelation to Say to us Today?

(1) Traditionally, the early church's engagement with the Graeco-Roman world has been understood largely in terms of persecution and martyrdom and the call to endurance. Today we are learning from studies of the social history of the first century of the Christian era that the church fought on a much wider front. Work on the political and socio-economic background of the Book of Revelation shows us the extent of the challenge faced by the communities for whom John wrote. By directing our attention not only to the suffering and persecution to be experienced by Christians in witnessing to the gospel but also to the cultural context in which they lived, John helps us address the challenges facing the church today.

(2) John is able to identify and analyse the principalities and powers because he has a theological critique to bring to bear upon them. This is made clear at the outset. We are shown God and his sovereignty over the world. God's

rule, far from being denied by the false values, evil and suffering in the world, is expressed in and through the life of the world. God entered history in the life of Jesus of Nazareth and overthrew the power of evil through the cross of Jesus Christ. The Lamb that was slain is the Lamb of God. His triumph is God's triumph. Hence it is God and the Lamb who are to be worshipped, not the evil Emperor. What was true of John's time is also true of ours. In its mission to the world the church has to develop a critical edge on culture. Without a critique formed from the gospel the church has little hope of assisting God's purpose of redeeming human life.

(3) John's vision offers us an alternative to the prevailing ideology. It is hinted at under various images throughout the book but it is not unveiled until the final section in the vision of the New Jerusalem. In preparation for this John describes its antitype. It is Babylon. Babylon stands for the Roman Empire. It is the earthly city of sin and evil which represents the dominant world order. In polarity to this city is another city. This city in turn symbolises a world order, the new order that will take the place of the present order. It is the holy city, the New Jerusalem, which descends from heaven to earth. Through the gates of this great metropolis flow the nations and commerce of the world. Because it is the city of God it provides healing and blessing for the nations. A world like ours, which is in danger of being worn down by evil or opting out of programmes and movements of reform, is thus offered the one thing which it needs more than anything else – hope.

(4) Fundamental to John's message to the churches is his vision. Strictly speaking it is a series of visions. But it is essentially *a* vision. It is meant to open eyes to the true state of affairs in society and to what God wills for it. Although John describes the vision as having been given to him in heaven by God it is not, so to speak, plucked out of the sky. As we shall find, it emerges from a very deliberate engagement of the word of God and the life of the world. Out of this engagement the vision emerges. It creates faith, conviction and commitment in those who embrace it. It subverts the existing culture.

(5) The Book of Revelation is an essential part of the New Testament. Without it we would be less prepared and equipped for Christian life and discipleship today. Of all the New Testament writings it is the most systematic exposé of evil and its power to deceive and enslave earth-dwellers. It also shows us how evil has been confronted and defeated. If John seems to overdo the danger facing his readers this is only because he aims to help them appreciate more fully the nature and scope of God's triumph and the important role which they themselves are called to play in it. The assurance of that triumph is the greatest feature of Revelation. It is a credible triumph because it is based upon a credible analysis. The Book of Revelation thus conveys the New Testament's message of good news.

VI
Christ and His Churches

Jesus Christ the Faithful Witness

The opening vision presents Jesus Christ as the faithful witness who calls upon the churches to continue that witness (1.5, 19-20). The Greek words from which we get martyrdom (*marturia*), translated as "witness" or "testimony" in English Bibles, keep reappearing throughout Revelation for the work of Christ and his followers. They refer to martyrdom as death and triumph and also testimony to this. How important it was to John to present Jesus as the witness *par excellence* can be seen from the repeated appellation of *marturia* to him (1.2,9; 12.17; 19.10; 20.4). The "witness of Jesus" is the witness he bore to God in his life and teaching and above all in his death. At a time when John's readers faced danger and the temptation to compromise, the portrayal of Christ as the protomartyr who was not afraid to pay the ultimate price of death for his testimony would have particular relevance. Christ is the exemplary martyr, the faithful and true witness to God, the one to whom the Christian communities of Asia Minor must look and emulate if they are to maintain their testimony and to conquer like him (12.11).

The way in which the testimony of Jesus is linked with prophecy in 19.10 shows that John believed that the witness of Jesus and his followers had a prophetic character. Viewed in the context of Revelation as a whole their testimony refers not only to predictions concerning the End but to a prophetic critique in the manner of the great prophets of the Old Testament. It is directed at the social and political order and also at the Christian community insofar as it shares the values of that order. This is undoubtedly the sense in which John understood his book to be regarded as prophecy (1.3) and his own role in maintaining the testimony of Jesus (1.2, 9). "You must prophesy again about many peoples and nations and languages and kings" (10.11). John, as we shall see, represents Christian witness as confronting the idolatry of the Roman Empire in a prophetic conflict and winning the nations to the worship of the true God (Bauckham, 1993b, 118-125).

The Seven Churches of Asia Minor

Before John says a word about the danger posed by the imperial cultus he addresses the churches. His feet are firmly planted on the ground and he never ceases to be concerned with life in this world. However difficult the times are, however uncertain the future is, there is no place for a slipshod and half-hearted church. Before John begins he has something to say which is essential to our understanding of his appraisal of the churches. He wants us to know that Christ is head of the churches; the churches belong to him.

Christ is depicted as present in the earthly congregations of his people. He sees to their needs, like a priest, attending the candles on the altar (1.13; 2.1). Whatever their shortcomings, the churches are in his hands (1.16, 20; 2.1). They are accountable to him and where necessary he will judge them (2.5); but he has died for them (2.8) and he loves them still (3.9, 19). He calls upon them to repent and promises them his blessings (2.7, 10, 16-17, 28; 3.5, 12, 20-21), That is their hope. Everything John has to say about the churches should be interpreted in the light of this fundamental fact.

The messages to the churches reflect the impending crisis. The church at Ephesus endures "patiently" (2.3), but it has lost its love – one of the signs of the End according to Matthew 24.12. Its future is thus under threat (2.5). Smyrna is facing suffering and imprisonment (2.10). Pergamum has had one martyr already (2.13), and is seriously endangered (2.14-15). Thyatira has endured patiently but it is tolerating those who advocate compromise (2.20). Sardis must awake to its danger (3.1-2). Philadelphia faces "the hour of trial" (3.10). The Christians of Laodicea are blinded by prosperity and totally unaware of their danger (3.15-18). But there is more to the crisis facing the churches.

The churches John describes occupied strategic positions in western Asia Minor. Asia Minor was foremost among the provinces in promoting the Emperor's cult. Its cities competed for the honour and status of erecting temples. The cult presented Jews and Christians with practical problems in their social and business dealings, especially as commerce and cult were linked in different ways (Kraybill, 1996, 123-141). Ancient temples had dining areas that served as restaurants for the guilds and other groups, and members of guilds would be expected to attend guild feasts. Ephesus was only one of many cities which had associations of craftsmen (Acts 19.23-27; Broughton, 841-844; Kraybill, 111-113). Inscriptions at Thyatira point to numerous trade guilds. At Corinth we find Paul declaring temples out of bounds (1 Cor. 8-9), even though he declared "we know that an idol has no real existence" (8.4, *RSV*). John condemns the food offered to idols at both Pergamum and Thyatira (2.14,20). All three code names he uses for abuses in the churches (Nicolaitans, Balaam, and Jezebel) very likely refer to accommodation to pagan society and moral compromise. The prosperity brought to the cities of western Asia Minor by Roman rule, which, as we shall see, seduced the citizens of the empire, contributed to problems within the churches (3.17-18).

The idolatry and fornication warned against in the messages to the churches (2.14, 20) are the dominant characteristics of the state that has usurped God's place (13.4, 14-18; 17.2-6). John's attack on "those who say they are Jews and are not" (2.9; 3.9) seems to point to the same basic problem. Jews, no less than Christians, are condemned for compromising their ancestral faith. By making accusations against Christians (slandering them), i.e., that they are not loyal to Rome, they are doing the devil's work. We shall find that the Beast blasphemes (slanders) both God and his people (13.6).

The crisis affecting the Christian communities of Asia Minor thus had to do not only with suffering and martyrdom, but with society at large. The pervasive influence of the idolatrous cult of Rome was making itself felt in these communities well before they were physically assaulted by the state. The crisis was compounded by its not being perceived to be a crisis. Roman rule represented peace and stability. Christians, along with others, benefited from the imperial rule, without being fully aware of the moral and ethical consequences. Consequently, the task facing John is not only unmasking the reality of life under Caesar but also alerting Christians to what it means for them.

John prefaces what he has to say with the words, "Listen to what the Spirit is saying to the churches" (2.7 etc.). This is pivotal to everything that follows. What it means is that God is addressing his church, and the church must pay attention. What the churches hear is not only judgement, but encouragement. The message is accompanied by the call to repentance and the challenge to endure and conquer with God's help (2.5-7, etc.).

God is still calling his church to listen to what he has to say to it. He tests its loyalty and questions its commitment. Despite its shortcomings, it is still his church. He is eager to give it new life, so that it will live faithfully and witness courageously.

VII
Worship God and the Lamb

John's vision properly begins with chapter 4. Along with chapter 5 it forms a carefully constructed literary unit. It begins with God and works out concentrically to embrace the whole of creation. The vision of God on his throne and the Lamb who opens the scroll, worshipped by the hosts of heaven and earth, is intended to provide John's readers with perspective on their situation. In virtually every chapter of Revelation the throne appears. This cannot be a coincidence. It is intended to alert readers to John's overriding theme of theocracy versus the rule of Satan, epitomised by the Emperor in the form of the Beast (2.13; 16.10; Ford, 1975, 76). The throne is the ultimate point of reference; it tests human allegiances. John loses no time in taking up the challenge posed for Christian faith by the ideology of the Empire and in describing the judgements which prepare the way for replacing the present evil world order by God's new world order of truth and righteousness.

One Seated on the Throne

First and foremost, our attention is directed to God on his throne (4.1-11). It would be difficult to find a stronger statement of the divine sovereignty. The rainbow spanning the throne points to God's providential rule over the whole of creation. John's readers need to hear about this rule. To live faithfully and courageously they must not only be made aware of the true nature of the situation in which they find themselves. They need above all to be able to see their situation in relation to the ultimate fact of life, namely, God ruling the universe. They need to be reminded that in the historic figure of Jesus Christ God took on and defeated the earthly forces threatening them. John has much to tell us about the way in which God exercises his rule on earth. For the moment, however, he is content to let us gaze in wonder at the symbols of God's majesty. Some of these symbols have political associations, others are distinctly liturgical, so it is possible to interpret the vision politically or liturgically. John merges the one with the other.

As befits the ruler of the universe, God is attended by a council. Twenty-four elders sit on thrones and wear crowns of gold. Nearby are the four living creatures, representing creation. Although scholars differ widely as to the identity of the elders and the four living creatures it seems likely that John means us to interpret them as the royal court, and to understand that the court is in session. In other words, God is exercising his sovereignty, notwithstanding what is happening on earth. The description of the elders as sitting may have in mind the practice of the Roman court. Whenever the Emperor heard legal cases orally he was seated and surrounded by senators, advisers and others. John's portrayal of the elders prostrating themselves in homage before the all-powerful ruler of the universe may reflect a well-established feature of royal courts in the ancient world. Obeisance before the ruler was an act of reverence that originated in Persia and became part of the ceremonial traditions of the Hellenistic kingdoms and eventually was incorporated into the imperial cult of Rome. John's description of the heavenly court bears such a striking resemblance to the Roman imperial court that David Aune thinks it must be a parody of the Emperor's court (1983, 12-20). Patently it is John's intention to portray the court and rule of him who is King of kings and Lord of lords, as far surpassing that of Rome (4.3; 5. 11). This is basic to John's attack on the absolutist claims being made for the Emperor.

The "sea of glass" before the throne (4.6) also carries political overtones: it reappears later as the barrier through which the martyrs have to pass in their contest with the Beast (15.2). Moreover, it is from the sea that the Beast rises to deceive the earth-dwellers (13.1-18). The "sea of glass" represents the cosmic sea over which God established his authority at creation (4.11; 5.13). By placing the sea in front of the throne John lets his readers know that God is aware of the kind of world over which he asserts his sovereignty and in which they are called to witness to the gospel.

Holy, Holy, Holy, is the Lord God, the Almighty

With the four living creatures the cultic and liturgical character of the scene predominates. The heavenly court takes on the appearance of a temple, filled with the praises of God. The four living creatures recall the seraphim in the temple vision of Isaiah 6 and the cherubim of Ezekiel 1. They are very likely intended to correspond to the cherubim that flanked the mercy-seat in the holy of holies of the earthly temple (Exod.25.18-22). They are beings whose entire existence is devoted to the worship of God. Their worship, extending out in ever-widening circles to include all the creatures of the entire creation (5.13), questions our loyalties. It points us to the true God who alone is to be served and worshipped. Such worship, far from being an escape from the horror of all that is happening in the world, arises out of this world. When the four living creatures cry "Our Lord and God" they are deliberately using political language of the day. Domitian demanded that his subjects acclaim him as "Lord and God" and participate in the imperial cult.

The Lamb who was Slain

How does God assert his sovereignty over the unruly world? How will he establish his kingdom on earth? These are the questions posed for the heavenly council. Hence the challenge of finding someone who is able to break the seals of the tightly sealed scroll. In the context of Revelation the scroll with the seven seals very likely refers to a document in which coming events are recorded (Dan. 10.21; 1 Enoch 81.1-3). Opening the scroll means causing these events to happen.

John is a dramatist as well as a theologian but he is not only heightening dramatic effect by having the entire universe searched for someone who is able to open the scroll, and then telling us that when no one could be found he was reduced to tears. There is a great deal more to the tightly sealed scroll. It represents the pain and frustration felt by all who suffer and have tried desperately to find redress without success. John's tears are the tears of all who care deeply about the wrongs of the world and long to see them put right.

Since John is so anxious to have the scroll opened it is fair to ask why he does not have God open it. That he does not do so, but has the Lamb open it, is an insight into his Christian understanding of God and the way God works. This is John's way of saying that Christ is the key to history. It is one of Revelation's many affirmations of the paramount importance of Jesus Christ. The hope Christ brings issues from what he has achieved as a human being no less than what he achieved as a divine being. This insight into the Christian understanding of God's way of working is brought out by George Caird, who says that God will not paternalise us by solving our problems for us.

> The divine decree waits sealed with seven seals, for the emergence of a human agent, willing and worthy to put it into effect, one who will place himself unreservedly at the disposal of God's sovereign will (1966,73).

John hears one of the elders announce Christ as "the Lion of the tribe of Judah, the Root of David" (5.5), but paradoxically what he *sees* is a Lamb bearing the marks of slaughter (5.6). When traditional Jewish expectation is turned into vision what we have is the Christian understanding of redemption. Precisely by juxtaposing such contrasting images, John mints a brand-new image: it is a victorious figure who conquers by self-sacrifice (Barker, 1996, 131-137). The Lion and the Root of David are Messianic titles. They evoke thoughts of a militaristic and nationalistic Messiah who delivers God's people and destroys their enemies (Isa. 11.1-5; Ps. of Sol. 17; 1 Macc. 3.1-9). The Lamb, by contrast, is vulnerable. He has suffered and died, and his death is what delivers people. John thus supplies us with a clue as to God's way of dealing with the destructive power at work in his world. The victory wrought by God through the suffering, death and resurrection of Jesus Christ becomes a leading theme of the book.

The Lamb is introduced as standing (5.6). He stands before the throne or indeed upon the throne, depending on how the Greek is interpreted. If John means that Christ is standing before the throne of God then we are probably intended to think of him as the victimised Christ appearing before the divine court as a suppliant, accusing the earthly powers of the injustices meted out not only to him and his followers but to all who have suffered wrong. He is the protomartyr, the forerunner of the many who will defy the authority of imperial Rome in the name of a higher authority (Reddish, 1988, 85-95). If, on the other hand, John means that the Lamb is standing upon the throne, that is, sharing it with God, then he is thinking of Christ as having been vindicated and enthroned by God. The Lamb is the martyrs' victor, the guarantee of the ultimate salvation of those whose robes are washed in his blood (7.14). In either case, what qualifies the Lamb to open the scroll are his sufferings and death as God's faithful witness, and his conquest of suffering, injustice, evil and death by his resurrection (cf. 12.1-6).

The good news that there is one who is able to open the scroll is greeted by the elders. The worship they offer the Lamb (5.8-14) is the same as that offered to God in the earlier vision (4.10-11). Virtually the same words are used in each case (5.12 and 4.11). What this means is that the Lamb shares the throne with God and shares the honours paid to God (cf. 5.13). There could be no clearer indication of the supreme importance attached to Christ. This high Christology is kept continuously in view throughout the entire book. We are told repeatedly that the throne is the throne of God *and of the Lamb* and that the worship given to God is also given to the Lamb.

Not to be overlooked is John's observation that the elders hold not only instruments of praise (harps) but also bowls full of incense. These, John tells us, "are the prayers of the saints" (5.8). This is the assurance that the prayers of those who cry out for justice on earth (6.10) are heard by God and will be answered (8.3-4). It is also the indication that Christ does not open the scroll independently of the prayers of his people.

In the liturgy of the elders more is told us about what it is that qualifies the Lamb to open the scroll. Firstly, the Lamb is worthy because he was slain (5.9). This strongly suggests that the Lamb is the lamb killed at the Passover (Exod. 12). The language of the second half of verse 9 and the following verse echoes the liberation of the Israelites from Egypt and their constitution as the people of God. However, the emphasis on the victory of the Lamb and the juxtaposition of the title 'Lamb' with 'the Lion of the tribe of Judah' and the Root of David in 5.5 are significant. Like the description of the Lamb as being horned and the representation of the Lamb as the leader of God's flock in 14.1-5, they suggest that the image uppermost in John's mind is the powerful horned sheep or ram which depicts the Messiah in Jewish apocalyptic (1 Enoch 89.42; 90.9). If the Lamb is the ram then we have one of the most remarkable examples of the rebirth of images that we find in Revelation, because the ram has been slain. The conqueror is a *sacrificial Lamb*. However we interpret the symbol of the Lamb, the important thing to note is that it is his death and the shedding of his blood which liberates people from their sins (5.9; cf. 1.5; 12.11). It is because of and not in spite of his death that he has become saviour.

The Lamb is also worthy because the people who are redeemed for God by his death become his treasured possession and are given their vocation. "You have made them to be a kingdom and priests serving our God" (5.10). John reminds his readers that their vocation continues, notwithstanding the dangers to which they are exposed. In telling us that those rescued by the

Lamb "will reign on earth" (5.10) John is giving us an important clue to what he will tell us later about the millennial kingdom (20.4).

The triumph of the Lamb reaches its climax in the acknowledgement of his worth by every creature in the universe (5.11-14). Redemption is placed at the heart of creation. John's apocalyptic teachers helped him to understand that since the rebellion of the human race had disastrous consequences for the whole of creation then its redemption must give hope to the whole of creation. Therefore every creature joins in the climax of praise. This is John's encouragement to all who long to see the world delivered from its pain and evil.

Once again John's subtext is clear. It is God and the Lamb who are to be offered worship, not Caesar. To worship anyone or anything else is idolatry. This is the first and fundamental challenge John issues to his readers. At the same time, the victory Jesus achieved through suffering and death is presented to the readers as a paradigm for Christian discipleship. Thus John's repeated calls to the churches to conquer, far from being undisguised imperialism, are summonses to the costliest form of discipleship.

A political message similar to that conveyed by John is to be found in the Heikhalot literature of Jewish rabbinic mystics of the third and fourth century AD. These Jews were intrigued by the vision of God's throne in Ezekiel 1 and set about describing the throne of God, the insignia of the royal office, and the enormous angelic company surrounding the throne. Implicit in their descriptions is a comparison between God and the Roman Emperor (Diocletian). Like John, they create an alternative symbolic universe for the purpose of encouraging the faithful to remain true to their beliefs in the face of the overpowering imperial ideology (Alexander, 1991, 276-297).

VIII
Maintaining the Testimony of Jesus

Having introduced his theme in chapters 4-5 John turns our attention to earth again. In chapters 6-16 he describes the judgements which are to be let loose upon its inhabitants. It is not easy to find one's way through these chapters. They share the problems we noted earlier concerning the structure of the book. John, however, does give some help to his readers by inserting literary devices into the text. Most obvious of these are the three cycles of seven: the seven seals (6.1-17; 8.1), the seven trumpets (8.2; 8.6-9.21; 11.15-19) and the seven bowls (15.1; 16.2-21). Each cycle is clearly numbered and has an identical link with the throne vision (cf. 8.5; 11.19 and 16.18-21). However the sequence is interrupted by three interludes, and it is difficult to see how the contents of the third interlude (chapters 12-14) fit into the overall structure. Moreover, there are all sorts of connections between these chapters. Some of these are clear, but others are not. Whether we view the three cycles of seven judgements as a chronological progression or a replay of the same event, John's intention is clear. The churches are to maintain their witness to Jesus notwithstanding the danger this will incur.

The sequence of seals, trumpets and bowls is initiated by the Lamb opening the scroll. The three cycles form a progression of disasters. Each conveys the same message, viz. the history of the world moves tragically on its degenerating course, but each describes it from a different point of view, with the result that when we come to the final cycle we have three accounts of how history reveals the divine judgement. But the fact that this chaotic and dangerous world is heading for judgement does not mean that God has given up on it. It is still owned by him. He wishes to save it and sends his servants to bear testimony to Jesus and his word.

Lord, How Long?

What witnessing to Christ may mean is made starkly plain in the interlude between the opening of the fifth and sixth seals. "I saw under the altar the souls of those who had been slaughtered for the word of God and the testimony they had given" (6.9). The suffering hinted at earlier in the book is now given full prominence. The martyrs John has in mind may be those who died in the persecution by Nero or those he believed would die in the coming ordeal. In any case, they are the clue to the meaning of the millennium. For the moment, it is their cry for vindication that John wishes us to hear (6.10).

Martyrs petitioning God for vindication is a familiar tradition in Jewish apocalyptic (1 Enoch 47.1-4; 4 Ezra 4.35-37). John tells us that they were put to death for their witness to God, thus linking them to the witness (*marturia*) motif of the book. Since he holds Rome accountable for "all who have been slain on earth" (18.24, *RSV*), the cry "Lord, how long?" (6.10) may well echo the cries of countless victims of oppression and injustice. What the martyrs ask for worries some modern readers who see it as a demand for personal vengeance, but when it is taken in the context of Revelation it is seen to be a plea for the vindication of God's rule and justice.

> With this cry they protest against the history of violence whose victims they have become, and call for its end; at the same time they defend themselves against any attempt to make sense of their death . . . there can be no question of suffering being given a meaning . . . but of re-moving what produces such meaninglessness, breaking off the history of violence (Wengst, 1987, 125-126).

God hears the cry of the martyrs. First, they are each given a white robe. That is to say, those who are condemned by the world are justified by God. The robes, as John will tell us at 7.14, are made white by the blood of the Lamb. Then the martyrs are told to be patient, to wait until they are joined by others who will seal their testimony by their deaths. This is a reminder of the crucial task of the church's witness. Whatever the hazards facing Christians, their witness to the gospel must continue. The earth is the theatre not only of God's judgements, but also of his grace. That is why the world is given the opportunity to hear the truth and repent.

The other group singled out in chapter 6 are those who represent the oppressive regime on earth. Attention is focused on the kings, magnates and the rich and powerful (6.15-17); they are the ones principally respons-ible for maintaining the empire's corrupt and illegitimate system. The disaster that overtakes them is an anticipation of the battle against the kings of the earth later in the book (19.17-19).

Modern readers frequently struggle to cope with John's accounts of the carnage and loss of life brought about by the overthrow of the enemies of God. Chapter 6 has introduced us to this; more is to follow. So perhaps this is the place to reflect on our reaction to it. It is possible to ease the problem by explaining the judgements that follow the apocalyptic horsemen as cata-strophes caused by human agents: war, famine, inflation and death. The earthquake can be attributed to nature. Similarly, the "wrath of the Lamb" (6.16) may be explained not as Christ's attitude towards the evil-doers but their fearful response to their end. More generally, the wrath or judgement of God has been taken to mean not the personal attitude of God towards wrongdoers, but an impersonal process of retribution working itself out automatically in history. But such attempts to distance God from the world are not only unsatisfactory but dangerous to faith.

If Revelation seems to highlight divine judgement rather than mercy, that is a message which an idolatrous generation needs to hear. If Mammon is our God, then the consequences of idolatry are manifest in the judgement to which we are consigned for our short-sighted self-interest. We live as part of an order in which injustice has distorted the way in which society and the whole created order functions. The world is out of joint, and that was most clearly demonstrated in the destruction of the Messiah by the representatives of the present scheme of things (Rowland, 1993, 83).

God's action in Jesus Christ is the sign of his concern for us. This concern explains why he reacts as he does to our sin and evil. It is the expression of his responsibility. It is the ultimate guarantee that this world remains God's world and even the most evil and rebellious within it are still God's humanity.

By depicting the injustice done to the martyrs and God's judgement on those responsible John introduces his story-line. When he has fully exposed the system responsible for the injustice he will reveal to his readers the better world of God's righteousness and justice and they will be asked to make a decision as to which order they will serve.

Those who have come out of the Great Tribulation

The blessings that God has in store for those who are faithful to the point of death are depicted evocatively in 7.9-17. The martyrs stand before the throne of God and the Lamb. This very deliberate focusing of attention on the martyrs indicates the central importance they have in the book. It is a preview of their vindication and future glory and is directly linked to the millennium.

The relation of this vision to what precedes it in 7.1-8, i.e. the sealing of the 144,000, has puzzled scholars. The martyr host is described as "countless" and as coming from every nation (7.9), whereas the first group is specifically said to number 144,000 and is from the tribes of Israel. The simplest solution is to take the countless host to mean Gentile Christians and the 144,000 to refer to Jews or Jewish Christians, but this would mean that it is only the latter who have divine protection since it is only they who are sealed (7.1-8). In 9.4 it is definitely the church as a whole that is sealed against the assaults of the demonic forces. If chapter seven is seen in relation to what John says about the conversion of the nations later in his book we find that the great martyr host who have survived the tribulation and the 144,000 are not two different groups but the same group, viewed in different ways. The 144,000 depict the church as owned and protected by God, while the countless host conveys God's promise to help the church not only to survive the crisis but also to witness to the gospel and win converts from among the nations.

The links connecting the two groups support this interpretation. The sealing of the 144,000 indicates that they are in need of God's protection in view of the coming ordeal, while the martyr host shows them as having survived martyrdom and standing victorious in the presence of God (7.14-15). The combat motif is present in both groups. The 144,000 recall the twelve tribes of Israel assembled for battle. Their numbering is a military roll-call (Num. 26.2; cf. 1.3, 20 etc.). The countless host has emerged victorious from the battle. Their white robes symbolise their victory (2 Macc. 11.8), while their palms remind one of the palms used by the victorious Maccabean warriors (1 Macc. 13.51).

Confirmation for this interpretation may be found in John's vision of the New Jerusalem at the end of his book. On the one hand, it is a clearly defined city, carefully measured and enclosed with twelve gates inscribed with the names of the twelve tribes of Israel (21.9-21); on the other hand, it is an enormous pilgrimage city, whose gates stand open to the nations (21. 24-26). The image of the compact twelve-fold city and the image of the sprawling metropolis are two ways of looking at the same thing.

The most important feature of the scene celebrating the triumphant passage of the martyrs through persecution has already been prepared for in the vision of the slain Lamb in chapter 5: it is the death of Christ. It is by means of Christ's death that the martyrs are victorious. "These are they who have come out of the great ordeal; they have washed their robes and made them white in the blood of the Lamb" (7.14, cf. 12.11).

The "great ordeal" (the Great Tribulation mentioned in 7.14) is not so much the danger of physical suffering and death as the maelstrom of conflicting loyalties. Those who have withstood the propaganda and blandishments of Rome and remain true to what God has shown them in Jesus Christ may be described as having "washed their robes and made them white in the blood of the Lamb" (Caird, 101).

Although the imagery has strong political and military associations, cultic motifs reappear. John fuses the thought of victory with that of purification by telling us that the redeemed have washed their robes white (cf. 19.8). Their purity, like their redemption, depends upon Christ having died for them, but this has not happened independently of them. They "washed their robes and made them white through the blood of the Lamb". The holiness of the martyrs reappears in 14.4-5 and is expressed once again in martial imagery. When John goes on to describe the triumphant martyrs as worshipping God "day and night within his temple" (7.15) he appears to be saying that they have been admitted to the holy of holies. If this is what he means then the rare honour accorded to the high priest once a year is their never-ending privilege. In this case the white robes worn by the redeemed may carry yet further meaning since white is the colour which was worn by the high priest when serving in the holy of holies (Mishnah *Yoma*, 3.6; 7.4). John who began by telling us that Christians serve on earth as priests (1.6; 5.10) now shows us the liturgical character of their heavenly life.

The Two Witnesses

After the preview of the vindication of those who are put to death John shifts attention to the scene of their earthly struggles. In chapters 8-9 the seven trumpets and the seven bowls are followed by a string of judgements which grow in intensity. In chapter 10 John's personal role as a prophet is recalled. He consumes the scroll he is given so that he may prophesy. Since the scroll is described as "open" (10.2), it is fair to assume it is the scroll opened in chapter 5. Chapters 11-13 contain a series of presentations leaving his readers in no doubt as to the nature of the struggle with the evil powers.

The martyrs reappear as the two witnesses (11.3-13). What is in store for them is indicated by the command that John receives to measure the temple, but to leave out its outer court. The passage in question is enigmatic. Jesus predicted that Jerusalem would be trodden down by the Gentiles (Lk. 21.24), but it cannot be the temple of Jerusalem to which John is referring: that now lay in ruins. It is more likely that John is describing the church and its protection by God. But what is meant by the "court outside the temple" and the "holy city" (11.2)? Some scholars suggest that the outer court refers to those in the church who are compromised or complacent. In this case the holy city must refer to the world outside the church. But that raises a new question: who is responsible for destroying the world? It is more satisfactory to follow Caird in thinking that it is the church throughout which is in mind (132). The temple is measured, i.e., the church is given an inner security against spiritual dangers. The outer court and the holy city are not measured because the church is not guaranteed immunity from bodily suffering or death. The holy city trampled by the Gentiles describes the church crushed by evil forces. This interpretation is confirmed by what follows.

The object of measuring the temple is to ensure God's protection for the two witnesses until they complete their testimony. The imagery and Old Testament allusions John uses to portray the two witnesses are complex, but the meaning seems clear enough. At 10.11 John was commanded to prophesy. At 11.3 the two witnesses are empowered to prophesy. The effects of such prophecy and its cost to those who deliver it are illustrated by what follows. The witnesses are protected by God while undertaking their work, but when their witnessing is completed they are killed by the Beast in the "great city" (11.8-10). But like their Lord, the witnesses are vindicated by God and raised to life. By introducing the Beast from the abyss into the story (11.7) John is not only preparing us for what is to come, but is making clear the intensity of the struggle waged against God's people. The story of the two witnesses then illustrates the meaning of martyrdom. It is at one and the same time the Beast's victory over the martyrs and their victory over the Beast.

IX

The Beast versus the Lamb

The Dragon and the Beast

It is time for John to explain the nature of the evil which is imperilling the world. He introduced this briefly when he mentioned the "great red dragon" who threatened to devour the newly born Messiah in chapter 12. Now in chapter 13 he describes the Beast. The Beast is the Roman Emperor (13.1), who has usurped the place of God and demands universal worship (13.4-18). Adela Yarbro Collins (1976) has made out an attractive case for believing that in representing the Emperor as the Beast in the battle with the Lamb John used a combat myth which appeared in a variety of forms in the Ancient Near East and the classical world and may be seen in the Old Testament (e.g. Isa. 27.1; 51.9-10 and numerous Psalms) and in Judaism (Qumran Thanksgiving Hymns 1QH11 (3) 3-18). These myths have a common pattern so that it is permissible to refer to them as "the combat myth". It has a recurring sequence of ideas:

– the existing order is challenged by a usurper often symbolised as a
    dragon or other beast
– chaos and disorder ensue
– a battle takes place
– the ruler is killed and the forces of evil cause mayhem for a time
– the legitimate ruler is restored to life again, goes to battle, reestablishes
    order and reigns supreme.

This myth is rewritten by John to convey his Christian understanding of the combat between good and evil. His aim is to help his readers understand better the nature of the struggle in which they are engaged. The Dragon who lies in wait for the birth of the divine hero Jesus is Satan himself (12.1-17). The battle fought out at the cross to overthrow the usurper is being re-enacted. God preserves the legitimate heir to the throne and he will rule the nations (12.5). Apocalyptic loved to draw correspondences between heaven and earth, and John's dramatic account of the war in heaven (12.7-9) is very likely to be understood as the cosmic counterpart of the victory of the Lamb on the cross.

Although the fierce onslaught on God's people and their final deliverance still lie in the future, John in his customary manner describes it as a *fait accompli*:

Now have come the salvation and the power
    and the kingdom of our God
    and the authority of his Messiah,
for the accuser of our comrades
    has been thrown down,

who accuses them day and night before our God.
But they have conquered him by the blood of the Lamb
and by the word of their testimony for they did not cling to life
even in the face of death (12.10-11).

John returns to the task in hand by explaining who the Beast is and why it is a threat to all. Chapter 13 thus marks an important stage in John's account of the conflict between truth and falsehood. In writing as he does about the Beast, John does not mean that the state as such is demonic, but that it becomes demonic when it makes absolutist claims for itself. It is when Rome becomes the Beast and the imperial city turns into a Harlot (17) that they are condemned.

John begins imaginatively by describing the Beast as "rising out of the sea" (13.1). This can allude either to the lair of the monster or to the arrival of the Proconsul over the horizon of the Aegean Sea on his annual visit to Asia Minor. In either case, Rome is clearly identifiable, especially when we take chapter 13 along with chapter 17, the other major passage about the Beast. In 17.9 the seven heads of the Beast are shown to be the seven hills on which the Harlot sits. Since the imperial city was universally known as the city built on seven hills John is making Rome's identity obvious. The Beast, which was not mortally wounded, as it appeared to be, but had been healed (13.3, 12, 14; cf. 17.8, 11) so that it is again in command, undoubtedly refers to Nero. Legend had it that Nero had not in fact died when he attempted suicide in AD68 but was in Parthia raising an army and would return to regain power (Sibylline Oracles 5.361-368). In line with this is the interpretation of the number of the Beast in 13.18 as a reference to Nero. (The numerical value of Nero Caesar in Hebrew is 666). Daniel 7, which John used for his picture of the Beast, was applied to Rome by Jewish apocalyptic (4 Ezra 12.10-30), so the way was prepared for John's use of Daniel as a prophecy of the danger facing God's people of his own day. Any further evidence we need for identifying the Beast as Rome is provided by John's remark that the Beast's authority extends over the whole earth (13.8, 12, 14).

Before we look at the use John makes of the Nero legend we need to consider the other beast he introduces in 13.11. Since the first Beast represents the Emperor, the second beast, described as coming from the land, must, therefore, refer to the local representative of the Emperor. Perhaps, alternatively, it might mean someone inside the churches (Balaam or Jezebel, according to Hemer, 1986, 122-123 and Garrow, 1997, 90-91) working subversively in the interests of the Emperor. In any event, the second beast derives its authority from the first one (13.12) and promotes its worship and suzerainty (13.15-17).

The pervasive influence of the Beast is emphasised (13.12, 15-17). Its control of trade and commerce is taken by some scholars as evidence of the penetration of the economic life of the cities by the imperial cult. Participation in the cult helped one to profit in the market-place and assist one's way into citizenship, but in the case of Christians it meant compromising their faith. If the danger to which Christians were exposed was being played down or ignored by some within the church, e.g. 'Balaam', 'Jezebel' or the 'false prophet' (2.14, 20-23; 16.13; 19.20), John's concern to expose the diabolical nature of emperor worship is all the more to the point.

John's determination to ensure that the churches understand the grave threat to which they are exposed reaches a climax in his portrayal of the Beast as the Antichrist. Thus the Beast was wounded and thought to be dead, but its death was followed by something which could pass for resurrection (13.3, 12, 14; 17.8, 11). Universal worship is given to it (13.4, 8). It performs signs and wonders (13.14). Its subjects bear his mark (13.17). It will return again (17.8c; cf.1.4; 4.8). We can say, therefore, that although John does not actually call the Beast the Antichrist he might well have done so. The name Antichrist appears in 1 John 2.18, 22; 4.3; 2 John 7 and has parallels in the "abomination of desolation" (*AV*) in Mark 13. 14 and the "lawless one" in 2 Thess. 2. 3-8. By deliberately contrasting the Beast with Christ John shows the ultimate evil of the ideology which had captured the hearts and minds of the Empire and those Christians who had compromised themselves.

In employing the combat myth and identifying the Empire as an idol John has delivered his strongest invective yet against the state. The power of Rome and the system it has established is not only fraudulent and a threat to order, peace and prosperity; it is a blasphemy against God. "It opened its mouth to utter blasphemies against God" (13.6).

John's description of the state as diabolical and the implacable enemy of those who worship God is highly subversive. If we should suppose that what he says refers only to the historical situation for which he wrote or to viciously oppressive regimes of our day, then our reading has failed to grasp what he is saying. John is addressing situations wherever Christians are faced by idolatry and the abuse of power in whatever form. His book should be considered to be essential reading for reflection on the Christian's response to such situations.

The Lamb to the Attack

Now it is the turn of the Lamb and his followers to wage war on the Beast. In chapters 12-13 the Beast was depicted as having successfully attacked the people of God (12.17; 13.7). In chapter 14 the 144,000 are assembled for battle on Mount Zion, the place of the Messiah's triumph over the hostile nations (Ps. 2.2-6; 4 Ezra 13.35-38). They are referred to as "those who have not defiled themselves with women for they are virgins" (14.4). The idea of men having to keep themselves free from defilement by women is offensive in modern Western societies, but the possibility that John was a misogynist or was following a cultic requirement enforcing sexual abstinence is unlikely. The combat myth used in the context makes it clear that in John's symbolic universe the virginity of the 144,000 is a metaphor. Soldiers preparing for war in Israel were required to abstain from sexual inter-course (Deut. 23.9-11; 1 Sam. 21.5; 2 Sam. 11.9-11). The way in which the 144,000 are described in 14.4-5 indicates that John thinks of them as a special group (martyrs) set apart by God. John should not be taken to mean that women and children are excluded from membership of the church or the warfare in which Christians are engaged, any more than the equiva-lent of the ritual purity in his mind, viz. moral purity (14.5), does not apply to everyone. The moral purity John refers to when he says that the faithful "have no lie in their mouths" is particularly apposite. The Beast is held responsible, above all, for the colossal lie it has used to deceive the world.

The 144,000 are the army of the Lord. These follow the Lamb "wherever he goes" (14.4). We have only to ask where the Lamb goes to see what John means his readers to understand. The Lamb goes to his death. Thus the disciples of Christ are called to follow him regardless of the cost (Aune, 1996, 274-277). This is a further pointer to the underlying theme of martyrdom.

The followers of the Lamb are also described as being without fault (14.5). We are told that those who endure are those who "keep the commandments of God and hold fast to the faith of Jesus" (14.12). In their contest with the falsehoods and deceptions propagated by the Beast (13. 13-14) it is necessary that Christians should not be compromised in any way. Integrity is essential. This is in keeping with the connection that the New Testament elsewhere makes between honourable conduct and mission (e.g.. 1 Pet. 2.12, 15, 19-20). John wants us to know that heroic acts of public witness to God's truth depend on countless apparently unheroic acts of personal integrity.

The intensity of the struggle in which the followers of the Lamb are en-gaged is emphasised by John's call to endurance (13.10; 14.12). Fiorenza brings out the particular nuance of the Greek word used by John (*hypomone*) by translating it as "staying power" (1985, 191). Endurance was extolled by Cynics and Stoics, but Aune is correct in believing that more akin to what John has in mind is the endurance attributed to the Jewish martyrs in 4 Maccabees (1997, 76). It is through their endurance that these martyrs conquer their tyrannical oppressor (1.11; 9.30; 15.30; 17.17,23). For John, endurance, like faithfulness and integrity, is a mark of those who follow the Lamb.

Out of the Sea Mixed with Fire

Since the previous vision of the martyrs depicted them as ready to take part in the Lamb's battle with the Beast (14.1-5) the vision of them beside the sea of fire assures us as to the outcome of the battle: it is based on the story of the deliverance of Moses and the Israelites from the Red Sea (Exod.15). The implied crossing of the Red Sea represents the martyrdom of the faith-ful and their arrival in the presence of God.

> I saw what appeared to be a sea of glass mixed with fire, and those who had conquered the beast and its image and the number of its name standing beside the sea of glass with harps of God in their hands. And they sing the song of Moses, the servant of God, and the song of the Lamb (15. 2-3).

The sea from which the martyrs victoriously emerge was introduced to us at 4.6. Its power to cause trouble is indicated by its description as set on fire. The savage deaths of the martyrs are not described: the flaming sea speaks for itself. Attention is concentrated on the praise offered by those who have survived death. "In the presence of God the martyrs forget themselves; their thoughts are absorbed by the wonders that surround them" (Swete, 1906, 193).

The hymn that the martyrs sing relates God's victory to the worship that the nations will offer to God. The martyrs praise God as "King of the nations" and look forward to the time when he will be worshipped by the nations. Already we are introduced to one of the features of the new age in the final vision of Revelation (21.24-26). As Bauckham says, the deliverance of the martyrs is not an end in itself, but serves to bring the nations to worship him "who alone is holy" (1993a, 306).

With this vision, the last series of judgements, the seven bowls, is about to begin (15.1, 5-6). Whereas persecution was the dominant theme of the previous series, the emphasis of this series is on judgement. John is telling us that the world moves inexorably and tragically on its ruinous way and it calls down upon itself the judgement of God.

Armageddon

The best known of the battles between the forces of good and evil in Revelation is Armageddon (16.12-16). Like so many other things in Revelation it is anticipated earlier (14.14). The word Armageddon is itself a puzzle. The most popular interpretation takes the reference to be to a mountain (*har*) of Megiddo (*magedon*). Megiddo was a famous battlefield from the time of Sisera's defeat (Judg. 5.19-20), but that is a plain. The nearest mountain is Carmel in the north, where the prophet Elijah had his battle with the priests of Baal in the time of Ahab and Jezebel (I Kings 18.19-46). It is best to suppose that John has created a symbol from different sources. What he is referring to is the build-up of evil and God's judgement on those responsible for it (16.17-21).

Armageddon has had a compelling fascination for writers fond of working out a date for the end of the world. Best known is Hal Lindsey's treatment in *The Late Great Planet Earth* (1970). Lindsey believed that the return of Jews to Palestine, following the setting up of the state of Israel in 1948, provided the datum line for working out the date of the End. He predicted that Armageddon would come when Russia fought with the Western nations in a battle in Israel, centred in the valley of Megiddo.

It is important to recognise that Armageddon is one of a number of battles described in Revelation. Similar accounts are found in 14.17-20; 19.11-21; 20.7-10. Their similarities raise questions we noted earlier in regard to the structure of the book. Is John describing the same battle that marks the End, or does he have in mind a series of battles leading to the End? We shall return to this question.

X
The End of Babylon

The fate which awaits the evil world order is at last described in chapters 17.1-19.10. John's message is about to reach its climax when this order is destroyed and replaced by a new order. His vitriolic attack on Babylon should be read in the light of his final vision of the New Jerusalem. Babylon and the regime it symbolises is responsible for the injustice, corruption and evil of the world; the sooner it is replaced by the New Jerusalem the sooner the earth will be relieved of all that harms it. This is why the old order must go. The destruction of Babylon is the judgement of God, but the lengths to which John goes in describing the make-believe world which Babylon has created for itself and the deception, exploitation and suffering resulting from it indicate that he believed that the awful fate it was storing up for itself owed as much to its own internal dynamics as to the judgement of God.

The Great Harlot

John's prophecy focuses on the city of Rome, but it has in mind the whole imperial order. Rome is the "great harlot" (17.1), the woman seated on seven hills (from early times a reference to the city of Rome)(17.9). Presently we are told plainly, "The woman you saw is the great city that rules over the kings of the earth" (17.18). Alongside the Harlot is the Beast (17.3, 8-11), which as we have seen, stands for Rome in terms of its military might. John tells us that the woman rides on the back of the Beast (17.3, 7). The idea is the same as that conveyed by saying that the woman is enthroned on the seven hills. It indicates that Roman civilisation is supported by Rome's military power. We have already been told about the nature of the Beast. Now we are to hear about the civilisation it maintains.

The personification of cities as harlots occurs frequently in the Hebrew scriptures. Not only Tyre and Sidon (Isa. 23.17; Nahum. 3.4) but also Jerusalem are so described (Isa. 1.21; Ezek. 16). Fornication is commonly used as a metaphor for any dalliance with paganism (Isa. 1.21; Ezek. 16.35-43; etc.). The figure of Jezebel appears in Revelation 2.20 as the sign of the church's compromise with the idolatry of the Roman cult. Thus in depicting Rome as a harlot John is passing judgement not so much on the physical and historical city as on what it stands for. But since he is a master at fusing images and creating meanings at different levels it is possible that the Harlot also refers to the goddess Roma. Roma personified Rome and was part of the cult. In this case John wishes his readers to know what the city's true character is. She is a prostitute. She has her name on her headband (17.5), like the prostitutes on the streets of Rome.

Although the woman is not worshipped like the Beast she has an autonomy of her own and is responsible for her corrupting influence on the peoples of the Empire. They are used and exploited by Rome, but cannot see this. The gorgeous clothes and jewellery worn by the woman (17.4; cf. 18.16) display the life-style she enjoys at her lovers' expense. The peoples of the Empire are led astray by the momentary enjoyment of Rome's rule – intoxicated by the draught from the Harlot's golden cup (17.2; 18.3).

The woman has more to answer for. She herself is "drunk with the blood of the saints and the blood of the witnesses to Jesus" (17.6). She treats them in exactly the same way as the Beast treats them (13.7). The distinction John makes between the woman and the Beast thus becomes blurred. Both are guilty of injustice; both will be judged by God (19.2, 20). The woman's evil results in her undoing. Not only the client rulers of Rome, but the Beast itself will turn against her, humiliate and destroy her (17.16-17). In time, they in turn will suffer a similar fate (19.19-21). "That which makes them live, that which gives them authority, that upon which they are based, is the very spirit that finally repudiates them, because it is the annihilator" (Ellul, 1977, 193).

The Doom of Babylon

Revelation 18 is a remarkable piece of writing, but it is only in recent times that its importance for understanding Revelation has been more fully appreciated. Modern studies of the mercantile and economic life of the Empire at the beginning of the Christian era show the significance of the economic critique of Rome in this chapter. Although chapter 18 differs in form from chapter 17 it is similar inasmuch as it deals with the civilisation of Rome rather than its military power. It carries the story-line of the book a stage farther in showing us Rome's nemesis. The actual destruction of the city is not described. That is left to our imagination. What we have are the reactions of those directly affected by the disaster. The chapter is in the form of a dirge or taunt song familiar to the Hebrew prophets. It is a work of art, full of pathos and irony.

The passage opens with an eerie depiction of the once great city. It lies silent. It is the haunt of demons and other repulsive creatures (18.2). This graphic reversal of Rome's fortunes is the result of liaisons with the nations (18.3; cf. 17.1-2). How this nefarious business started is now explained: the merchants of the earth made their fortunes from their affairs with the Harlot (18.3).

Following the familiar use of fornication in the Old Testament for Israel's worship of foreign gods, John's criticism of Rome has to do, in part, with its promotion of the imperial cult. The major cities of Asia Minor all bore the coveted title of "temple warden" for the Emperor. It is no surprise that John singles out the maritime trade of the Empire for censure, since every port has its temple (Kraybill, 123-131). At an earlier stage John told us that no one could "buy or sell" without acknowledging the divinity of the Emperor (13.17). Here he attacks the ship-owners, merchants and the client kings of the provinces for their affairs with the Harlot (18.3,9; 19.2), i.e., participating in the cult.

John's attack on Rome also relates to its economic exploitation of the Empire and the political and military power that supported it. By establishing peace and stability in the Mediterranean world Rome had made possible the growth of a vast trade, which resulted in prosperity for those who were in a position to seize the opportunity created. It was the provincial elites who prospered, "the kings of the earth", the merchant classes and ship owners. The powerful of the earth have grown rich through connivance with the system (18.3, 15, 19). For the masses it was a different matter: they lived in poverty and slavery. According to the economic historian of the Roman Empire, Mihail Rostovtzeff, there was a continuous struggle between the rich and the poor in Asia Minor from the time of Emperor Vespasian (1957, I, 98-99, 204-209). Roman writers were themselves concerned about Rome's treatment of the provinces. We find Juvenal urging those appointed to service in the provinces to "have compassion on the impoverished provinces whose very bones have been sucked dry of marrow" (*Satires* 8. 87-90; Petronius, *Satyricum* 119; Wengst, 35-37). Already at 9.21, where John makes clear the substance of the charges he is bringing against Rome, theft is included in the list.

In John's enumeration of the imports which flooded into Rome the emphasis is on luxury items and is intended to draw attention to the opulent and extravagant lifestyle of the upper classes of the city. But there is worse to follow. Rome traded in the bodies and souls of slaves, which are treated as articles of merchandise (18.13). Rome is responsible not only for the deaths of Christians but for all whose lives were the price of her acquiring and maintaining power (18.24). Like Tacitus, John is well aware that the *Pax Romana* was "peace with bloodshed" (*Annals* 1. 10.4; Wengst, 10).

The vast range of imports and the extensive trading network in the Empire of John's day is clear from his bill of lading:

Cargo of gold, silver, jewels and pearls, fine linen, purple, silk and scarlet, all kinds of scented wood, all articles of ivory, all articles of costly wood, bronze, iron, and marble, cinnamon, spice, incense, myrrh, frankincense, wine, olive oil, choice flour and wheat, cattle and sheep, horses and chariots, slaves – and human lives (18.12-13).

Similar lists are to be found in Virgil (*Georgics* 1.56-59) and Pliny (*Natural History* 37.204). Aelius Aristides declared that if people cannot find what they are looking for in Rome they can be certain it is not obtainable elsewhere (*Oratio* 11). Whilst John's list includes essentials like food and other things, his concentration on luxury items shows that he was intent on exposing the wealth and extravagance of life in Rome (Bauckham, 1993a, 352). John makes no attempt to conceal his disdain for the way the rich of Rome lived (18.14).

The inclusion of wheat in John's list points to the enormous enterprise of keeping Rome supplied with food and the wealth it generated for the ship-owners. Some 400,000 tons of grain were shipped annually to the city. The provinces might pay high prices for grain and sometimes go without, but no effort was spared in meeting the needs of the inhabitants of Rome. About 200,000 families received a regular handout of grain. The political importance of ensuring that the city was supplied with food resulted in numerous privileges being granted to ship-owners. The Emperor Claudius, at a time when Rome had a perilously low supply of grain in reserve in AD41, increased the benefits enjoyed by the ship-owners. He awarded them subsidies for building new vessels and undertook to indemnify the cost of ships lost at sea. Additional privileges were granted by Nero and Hadrian. Contemporary texts provide evidence of the vast sums of money made by ship owners supplying Rome (Kraybill, 102-110). Consequently we are not surprised that John tells us that the merchants and seafarers grew rich from their trade with Rome (18.3, 15, 17) or that the destruction of Rome caused shock and distress to those who profited from its great commercial enterprise.

> The kings of the earth, who committed fornication and lived in luxury with her, will weep and wail over her when they see the smoke of her burning; they will stand far off, in fear of her torment. . . . And the merchants of the earth weep and mourn for her, since no one buys their cargo any more...and all shipmasters and seafarers, sailors and all whose trade is on the sea, stood far off and cried out as they saw the smoke of her burning, 'What city was like the great city?' "

And they threw dust on their heads, as they wept and mourned, crying out,
> Alas, alas, the great city,
>> where all who had ships at sea
>> grew rich by her wealth! For in one hour she has been laid waste (18.9-10, 17-19).

John seems anxious that the disaster should be appreciated as fully as possible. He proceeds to tell us what the loss of Rome means to the arts, human life and society. This great city which concentrated in itself all human activity, this centre of aesthetic pursuits and honest endeavour, this place where human love found its fulfilment, has fallen silent (18.22-23).

Caird suggests that for all John's criticism of Rome he had a genuine appreciation of the city and anguish over its destruction (227. Cf. Rowland, 143). By contrast, Boesak, writing in the apartheid era of South Africa, says that the cries heard by John were not those who benefited from oppression and exploitation but those who suffered from it, "Rejoice over her, O Heaven, you saints and apostles and prophets! For God has given judgement for you against her" (1987, 122).

Bauckham also takes issue with those who believe that the text shows admiration for Rome and the huge mercantile enterprise that contributed to its greatness. He believes John laid a "hermeneutic trap" in the distress of all whose livelihood was lost by the fall of the city.

Any reader who finds himself sharing that perspective – viewing the prospect of the fall of Rome with dismay – should thereby discover, with a shock, where he stands, and the peril in which he stands. And for such readers, it is of the utmost importance that, prior to the picture of the mourners, comes the command:

> Come out of her, my people, lest you take part in her sins, lest you share in her plagues (*v*. 4) (Bauckham, 1989, 99; 1993a, 376).

From our study of the churches in Revelation 2-3 we saw that their members were by no means all poor. Some were affluent and in the pursuit of the material and social benefits of Roman rule had compromised themselves. John's call to them to have nothing to do with Rome and all that it stood for would therefore come as a stinging rebuke. Nowhere is John's challenge to his readers to wake up to the reality of the situation clearer than in Rome's arrogant and proud boast that it is impervious to the ravages of time:

> I rule as a queen;
> I am no widow,
>   and I will never see grief (18.7).

The ability of the Empire to survive the most appalling disasters (e.g., the year of the four emperors, AD68-9) and the absence of any serious challenge to its rule had resulted in paranoiac delusions of grandeur. It was a matter of the greatest urgency to John that his readers sever their alliance with this deranged megalomaniac. Judgement would fall not only on Rome but on all who shared its guilt.

What the Spirit is saying to the Churches

John's passion for justice in chapters 17-18 is expressed in terms which challenges us to consider what is happening in our world today. Comparisons run the risk of being simplistic; serious analysis of our economic order is essential. However, there are obvious similarities between our economic order and that described by John which invite comment.

What John says about the way in which the system works to the advantage of some and to the disadvantage of others has a clear parallel in what is happening in the global economy. Like the rule of Rome, the market is a law to itself. It favours elites and does little to improve life for those most in need of help. It is responsible for widespread oppression and injustice. The market has the power to deconstruct communities, making workers expendable commodities, and leaving society to cope with family and community breakdown and the despair and violence which are its inevitable consequences. We are told that the widening chasm in the distribution of wealth between rich and poor in many countries is the regrettable but necessary price of changes that have to be made. The human cost of the debt crisis and trade tariffs to the developing countries in terms of infant mortality, cut-backs on health care, education and agricultural development is creating a disaster on a scale the world has not yet witnessed. The trafficking in human souls described in the Book of Revelation calls in question the way in which we run our world today.

Similarly, John's description of the luxury imports and the wasteful life-style of Rome cannot but cause us to reflect upon aspects of our consumer society. An economy fostering the belief that human beings are defined by taste and style and what they wear and advertising which uses coercion and seduction to create needs should hear what John says about "fornication", i.e., shortcuts to personal gratification. We have to ask what the much-vaunted choice of the consumer age means in a society where people do not have the means to make choices. They are "outcasts from the consumer society's banquet" (Serge Latouche).

Since John's concern for the victims of injustice begins with those who suffer for their religious beliefs what he says cannot but remind us of those who suffer for their faith today. More Christians and people of other faiths have been put to death during the 20th century than in any previous period in the history of the church. It is ironic that our postmodern world, with its emphasis on pluralism and dialogue, has witnessed growing prejudice, intolerance, torture and killings. Religion is used to support ethnic and nationalistic aspirations and members of one faith persecute and murder those of another faith. The statues installed on the west front of Westminster Abbey in 1998 in memory of the martyrs of the twentieth century are a timely reminder of an injustice that too few people today are aware of. Nor should our concern for the victims of injustice stop there. John's concern extended to "all who have been slain on earth" (18.24). The corollary of John's belief that God's sovereignty extended to everyone obliges us to discover what the Spirit is saying to the churches about injustice wherever it appears and whatever form it takes and see this in relation to John's concern for vindication of the oppressed.

Whatever the nature of the struggle in which people find themselves today in the alleviation of suffering, injustice and oppression what the Book of Revelation says about the need for endurance or staying power is particularly relevant. The immensity of the issues, the failure of well-intentioned programmes and the contemporary desire for quick returns all test the resolve of those who are working for change. The staying power necessary to sustain commitment in the face of such challenges is urgently needed. John believed that such staying power derived ultimately from the vision of the Lamb before the throne. The wounds he bore were testimony to his endurance. Following the Lamb, therefore, means emulating him in enduring suffering and, if need be, death.

XI
Christ Comes with the Armies of Heaven

The fall of Rome does not in fact mark the end of all evil. Satan, the malevolent power behind the throne, still has to be taken in hand. More gruesome pictures of the destruction of evil appear in chapters 19-20. The writer's apparent fascination for depicting a violent end to evil troubles many present-day readers. Even though we know that in John's mind the well-being of the world depends upon evil being put down and truth and goodness vindicated we are scarcely prepared for the carnage and death which we find in these chapters. Even when we make allowance for the symbolic nature of John's writing the problem remains.

The vision of Christ sweeping down from heaven on a white horse with the saints also riding on white horses to make war on all evil-doers, followed by the capture of the Beast and the False Prophet in 19.11-21 has traditionally been understood as John's account of the Second Coming of Christ (for a recent scholarly presentation see J.Webb Mealy, 1992). Furthermore, many readers and commentators on Revelation have interpreted the Second Coming as the prelude to the millennium in 20.4-6. The fact that Christ is described as descending to earth *before* the millennium gave rise to the premillennial school of thought.

Premillennialists connect Revelation 19-20 with passages from the synoptic gospels and Paul's writings relating to the Second Coming. Thus Christ is expected after the period of turmoil and suffering described in such passages as Mark 13 and 2 Thessalonians 2. This is believed to refer to the "great tribulation" in Revelation 7.14. Paul's words about believers being "caught up in the clouds... to meet the Lord in the air" (1 Thess. 4.17), described as a secret "rapture" or "taking away" of the faithful, are believed to be an account of the way in which Christians alive at the End would be spared the tribulation predicted in Revelation. Believers who have died (1 Thess. 4.16; 1 Cor. 15.52-56) are to be raised to life and share in Christ's rule over the unbelieving nations for a thousand years (Rev. 20.4). Different eschatological predictions are thus brought together to produce a comprehensive End-time prophecy.

This is a classic case of interpretations of scripture resulting from the harmonisation of texts from different parts of the New Testament without regard to their contexts. How Revelation 19.11-21 came to be understood as referring to the Second Coming as elsewhere described in the New Testament is difficult to understand. It is clear beyond all doubt that John's interest in this passage is not in the faithful but in the wicked (Marshall, 1968, 337). In any case, the faithful are already in heaven and are not thought of as transported there as in Parousia texts. Attempts made by some scholars to get round this difficulty by interpreting the armies accompanying Christ as angels (which we find associated with the Parousia in other texts) are singularly unconvincing, since their clothing ("fine linen, white and pure") unmistakably identifies them as martyrs (19.14, cf. 6.11; 7.13-14; 19.8). Furthermore, Revelation does not have familiar Parousia features like the coming of Christ on the clouds (1.7; Matt. 24.30; 26.64; Mk. 13.26; 14.62; Lk. 21.27), accompanying angels (Matt. 13.41,49; 16.27; 24.31; 25.31; Mk. 8.38; 13.27; 2 Thess. 1.7) and the gathering in of the elect (Matt. 24.31, 40-41; Mk. 13.27; cf.Matt. 13.41, 49; 1 Thess. 4.17; 1 Cor. 15.52).

It is clear that John expected the Parousia (1.7; 3.11; 22.7, 12,20), though the coming of Christ he has in mind in some passages refers not to a world-wide coming but a local one, i.e., to a particular church (cf. 2.5, 16, 25; 3.3; Caird, 32, 41). What John says about the Second Coming does not have a great deal of detail. From the language he uses ("coming with the clouds" (1.7) and "coming like a thief" (3.3; 16.15) it is, however, evident that he was familiar with the Parousia traditions in the New Testament (Matt. 24.30 etc. and par.; 24.43; Lk. 12.39-40; 1 Thess. 5.2; 2 Pet. 3.10). But the descent of Christ to earth pictured in 19.11-21 connects not with these traditions but with John's own particular concerns. It belongs to his theme of the holy war. The martial character of Christ's mission is emphasised by his riding on a white horse (a feature not mentioned anywhere in the New Testament in connection with the Second Coming) and by his sword and rod of iron. Earlier we were told that the faithful "follow the Lamb wherever he goes" (14.4). The Lamb goes to war (19.11), and his followers go with him. He is armed. His sword is the word of his mouth (19.15); hence his name is "the Word of God" (19.13). The battle ensues. The forces of evil are overpowered through faithful witness, not force of arms. This is a replay of the battle that was fought and won on the cross. The martyrs conquer because they share in what Christ accomplished on the cross: the white robes they wear have been washed in the blood of the Lamb.

There is a "coming" described in 19.11-21, but it is one of many such comings in the book. The descent of the heavenly agents to earth to execute judgement is a major theme running throughout the whole of Revelation. In 10.1-3 John sees a mighty angel "coming down from heaven" and taking over land and sea by planting his feet upon them. In 14.14-20 the "one like the Son of Man" reaps the harvest of the earth's wickedness. Similarly, in 18.1 an angel, who illuminates the earth with his glory, is described as "coming down from heaven" to announce the fall of Babylon. And in 20.1 an angel who has the key of the abyss "comes down from heaven" to bind Satan. Since the coming of Christ to earth in 19.11-21 is part of a recurring theme it should not be singled out for special emphasis. It has to do with the ongoing battle against evil. This conclusion holds true whether one interprets the battle in question as a recapitulation of the one End-time battle or thinks of several battles arranged in chronological sequence.

The prominence given to the descent of the "armies of heaven" shows that this was of equal importance to John. It is significant that Christ's descent is interrupted for the purpose of introducing the warrior host (19.14). What we have here is another of John's portrayals of the vindication of the martyrs. Recent scholarship has done students of Revelation a great service by painstakingly showing the extensive literary links connecting the different parts of the book. Thus 19.11-21 is connected with the preceding chapters, especially 13-16. It is a characteristic of John's to present the same reality under different images. The "armies of heaven" who accompany Christ on his mission to earth are none other than the followers of the Lamb who were conquered by the Beast in chapter 13 (cf. 19.20 and 13.7, 15) and who were raised to life and assembled for battle again in chapter 14. Symbolic of the conflict in which they are engaged is the battle fought at Armageddon at 16.12-16. Another such battle is described in 17.12-14, in which, significantly, the warrior Lamb is described as accompanied by his followers (17.14). The Christ who treads the winepress of God's fury in 19.15 is the "one like the Son of Man" whose sickle reaps the evil harvest of the earth at 14.14-20. In similar fashion, the Christ from heaven who smites the nations in 19.15 is followed by yet another heaven-sent means of judgement on the opponents of God in 20.9.

The vision of Christ on his white horse accompanied by his followers on white horses, descending to earth to execute judgement on evil doers, is one of numerous mythical battle scenes, conveying one thing: humanity is accountable to God and those who commit evil will be judged, while those who have been wronged will be vindicated. The fact that one of these battles (19.11-21) occurs just before the millennium does not entitle us to single it out and give it prominence over the rest. As we noted, a further battle is waged *after* the millennium (20.7-10). The definitive end is not the victory of Christ and his army over the Beast and the false prophet in 19.11-21, but, as we are presently to see, the destruction of Satan, and this does not happen until after the millennium (20.7-10). It is the binding of Satan that is more directly responsible for the ushering in of the millennium than the descent of Christ and his armies to earth. Too often chapter 20 is read as if it marks a break in the narrative at the end of chapter 19. In fact, these chapters are a unified whole; the break does not come till chapter 21.

Before we proceed to the vision of the millennium it will help to summarise our findings thus far. John begins by putting the crisis faced by the church in theological perspective (4-5). He then proceeds to show the judgements of God working out in history (6-16). The visions of the seals, the trumpets and the bowls all convey the same message. The reader is thereby trained from the outset to expect to find the one and the same reality being conveyed under different images and viewed in different ways. The Beast attacks the saints (13). Then it is the turn of the Lamb to attack the Beast. Hence the army of the Lord is assembled in readiness on Mount Zion (14.1-5). There follows a series of symbolical battles, beginning with Armageddon (16.12-16) and including the conquering Christ and his army from heaven

(19.11-21). These battles are to be understood in terms of the great cosmic conflict for the sovereignty of the world fought between God and the forces of evil. This conflict, which begins with the Beast, includes but does not end with the attack of Christ and the armies of the Lord on their white horses. It continues after the millennium until Satan himself is destroyed (20.7-10). Like the series of seals, trumpets and bowls, the battle-scenes all depict the judgement of God. To attempt to interpret the "coming" of 19.11-21 in terms of the Second Coming, with the removal of the faithful from the earth, is quite out of sympathy with the great interest taken in the earth in Revelation. The only way in which John thinks of the faithful being removed from the earth is through martyrdom.

Traditional interpretation of 19.11-21 in terms of the Parousia maintained that the coming of Christ to earth was to establish the millennium. There is a connection between Christ's coming in this passage and the millennium in the next chapter of Revelation but it is not such a direct one as has habitually been maintained. If anything is to be singled out as preparing the way for the millennium it is the binding of Satan. But it is wise not to look for a single event, since the millennium or the vindication of the martyrs belongs to a theme occupying the whole of Revelation.

Once the connection between the millennium and the Second Coming is broken it follows that all discussion on premillennialism, postmillennialism and timetables for dating the End falls away. In any case, the millennium has to do with other concerns. What John says about it precludes our making it part of a programme for the winding up of history.

To sum up. The descent of the divine warrior and his troops to punish evil-doers belongs to the conflict motif of chapter 14 and following chapters. All the while John depicts the different engagements in the battle between good and evil he is at the same time describing how the tables are turned on the corrupt city and the regime it represents. The city is judged and found wanting (17) and destroyed (18). Presently John will describe the capture and destruction of Satan, and tell us how "the kingdom of the world has become the kingdom of our Lord and his Messiah".

The gruesome language used to describe the overthrow of evil-doers in chapter 19 should not be allowed to detract us from the underlying message, viz. the weak and powerless of the earth do not have to endure victimisation and oppression for ever. Evil is not invincible. Justice will triumph. John will not have us become fatalistic about the future of the world but hope for the overthrow of evil, the establishment of a just order and the recompense of all who have suffered unjustly.

XII
The Millennium

Then I saw thrones, and those seated on them were given authority to judge. I also saw the souls of those who had been beheaded for their testimony to Jesus and for the word of God. They had not worshipped the beast or its image and had not received its mark on their foreheads or their hands. They came to life and reigned with Christ for a thousand years. (The rest of the dead did not come to life until the thousand years were ended.) This is the first resurrection. Blessed and holy are those who share in the first resurrection. Over these the second death has no power, but they will be priests of God and of Christ, and they will reign with him for a thousand years (20.4-6).

All sorts of questions suggest themselves. Is it only those who suffer death for the testimony of Jesus or all the faithful who are resurrected to share with him in the millennial reign? Where are the martyrs vindicated? In heaven or on earth? Why is Satan released to cause further trouble after the millennium (20.7-9)? Why should the enemies of righteousness appear (in the form of Gog and Magog) when they were supposedly destroyed (19.11-21). What is the relation of the millennium to the new heaven and the new earth in the final part of the book (20-22)?

The millennium itself poses particular questions. Should it be taken at face value as a description of an actual period of history as students of the Bible have understood it from the earliest times? Or is it a symbolical representation of the eternal rule of Christ and the saints, as Augustine and others have taken it to mean? What significance should we attribute to the fact that the millennium is nowhere else described in the New Testament?

Many of the questions surrounding the millennium fall away or find an answer in the now widely held view that John was addressing the political ideology which undergirded the empire and preparing the church to engage in the dangerous task of attacking it. It is against this background that the millennium, like everything else in Revelation, is to be viewed.

Throughout his work John has been alerting the churches to the threat posed by the imperial cult and calling them to engage in the perilous mission of attacking it in the name of a higher loyalty. He reminds his readers that it is God who rules the world and he alone should be worshipped. In and through Jesus Christ God has taken on the powers of evil and defeated them. The millennium is the disclosure of God's triumph over evil. This is dramatically portrayed by the binding of Satan, which prepares the way for the reign of Christ and those who lay down their lives in the battle against evil.

The costliness of witnessing to God's rule is acknowledged throughout

Revelation, and John makes a sustained effort to show that it will have its reward. Those who overcome the deceptions and temptations of their culture will eat the fruit of the tree of life (2.7). They will receive the crown of life and escape the second death (2.10-11). They are promised the "hidden manna" (2.17) and great power and influence (2.26-28). Those who conquer will be robed in white and have their names inscribed in the "book of life" (3.5). They will become pillars in God's temple (3.12) and share the throne of God and the Lamb (3.21). They will reign on earth (5.10). Those who survive the Great Tribulation will engage in the never-ending worship of God, beyond the reach of want or sorrow (7.15-17). Those who overcome the Beast will sing the praises of God (15.2-4). They will join the conquering Christ in putting down evil on earth (19.14). Now they are promised a part in Christ's millennial kingdom (20.6). The thought once more is of the faithful participating in Christ's victory. Because Christ has been raised they will be raised; because Christ reigns they will reign. It is thus clear that what the millennium signifies is integral to John's attack on the imperial system and the encouragement he gives to those who challenge it. What it says about Christians sharing in the victory of Christ on the cross and in his resurrection is essentially the message of the New Testament at large.

In using the idea of an interim messianic age John shows his indebtedness to Jewish apocalyptic (2 Baruch 39.7-40.3; 4 Ezra 7.28-29; cf. Apocalypse of Elijah 5.36-39; Sanhedrin 99a). It is important to note, however, that it is a purely formal dependence. No sooner has John taken over the concept than he invests it with his own very distinctive meaning by linking it with the victory of Christ and the vindication of the martyrs. The millennium in Revelation is a specific response to a specific situation. It is when the millennium is taken out of its context of martyrdom in Revelation that all sorts of problems arise. As Bauckham says of attempts to understand the millennium in Revelation, without reference to its function in relation to the martyrs, but taking it to refer to an event in the future:

> Once we take the image literally – as predicting an actual period in the future history of the world – it is impossible to limit it to this function. We then have to ask all the questions that interpreters of Revelation ask about the millennium but which John does not answer because they are irrelevant to the function he gives it in his symbolic universe (1993b, p.108).

It is necessary to remind ourselves once again that John writes in a highly symbolical way. The thousand-year reign can no more be taken literally than the ten-headed and seven-horned monster. What the imagery is meant to convey is what we have to decipher, and that can only be properly undertaken within the historical setting of Revelation and its particular aim.

The question whether the millennium is for martyrs only or for all the faithful, which moderns often ask, probably never entered John's head. He wrote his book to help those for whom martyrdom was a very real possibility.

He was not thinking of others. Had we had the opportunity of questioning him he would no doubt have conceded that not all the faithful would die as martyrs. In any event, all the faithful have a place in the New Jerusalem irrespective whether they had a part in the millennium or not. As we shall see, multitudes enter its gates, and they do so not because they managed to get themselves martyred but because Christ died for them (22.14; cf. 1.5; 7.14; 12.11; Mealy, 113-114).

Another question debated by some scholars is the location of the reign of the martyrs. Some take it to be earth; others think it is heaven. The matter should not be in any doubt, for the context contains enough information for us to see that it is the earth that is intended. Firstly, the binding of Satan has meaning only if it refers to the trouble that he causes on earth. Secondly, the role of priests given to the saints during the millennium implies that they function on earth. This conclusion is in fact indicated at the outset. As early as 5.10 we are told that the faithful are priests and that they will reign on earth. Thirdly, when the period of the millennium is over and the struggle between good and evil has resumed, with the forces of Gog and Magog surrounding the camp of the saints and the beloved city (20.9), it is implied that the millennium is on earth.

Throughout Revelation it is the earth which is the place where God's sovereignty is challenged and suffering is caused to the followers of the Lamb and countless others (18.24). It is on the earth, therefore, that God will vindicate his sovereignty and champion the cause of all who have suffered unjustly. For this reason the binding of Satan prefaces the millennium. It is of the greatest possible significance for John's readers to know that the kingdom of this world is to become the kingdom of our Lord and his Messiah (11.15). Justice must not only be done, but be seen to be done. The same point will be made with still greater emphasis in the final vision of the New Jerusalem descending to earth. The thousand-year reign of Christ and the saints anticipates the transfer of the throne of God and of the Lamb from heaven to earth (22.3).

But John is concerned to show that the millennium means more than recompensing the faithful for the injustices and miseries they suffer. It also signifies the continuation of their divinely given vocation as priests (20.6; cf. 1.6; 5.10). How John envisaged their undertaking their ministry in the millennium is not clear, but since priesthood is always exercised on behalf of others R.H. Charles is probably correct in suggesting that the saints carry out their ministry in relation to the nations (1920, II, 186; cf. 143). The conversion of the nations is depicted in the final vision of the book.

If the foregoing exposition is correct then the fact that the millennium is of a limited duration and is followed by renewed conflict should not be the problem it has often been for readers of Revelation. John wants us to know that while life on earth continues the struggle between good and evil continues. The release of Satan and his further deception of the nations and the rampaging armies of Gog and Magog all convey realism and insight. They speak to us of the resilience of evil and its capacity to cause trouble, and remind us of the fact that the inhabitants of the earth never cease to depend upon divine help.

But before John concludes this part of his work it is equally important for him to show that the battle between good and evil does not last for ever. It has an end. Truth and goodness prevail. Hence Satan follows the Beast and the False Prophet into the lake of fire (20.10). There follows the Last Judgement (20.11-15). The Great White Throne, before which everyone appears, indicates the accountability of human beings for their conduct. It also points to a universal justice. All are judged by what they have done (20.13).

All this means that we need to be very critical of popular interpretations of the millennium in the Book of Revelation. It is time to strip the millennium of the utopian fantasies and other accretions it has acquired through the ages. Visions of the lion lying down with the lamb and the destructive fanaticism of militant millenarian movements are based on the mistaken view that John's vision of the millennium is to be taken literally. But they do have this in common with John: God is sovereign and the earth shall have peace and not tyranny. The great importance John attached to the earth in his understanding of God's purposes is re-emphasised, as we shall see, in his vision of the New Jerusalem. There is nothing here of the world-denying predictions of Doomsday prophets frequently associated with the End. This means that we cannot hope to rehabilitate John's millennium vision without a world-affirming vision and commitment to witnessing to God's rule and to helping those who are denied justice. This is not the same thing as saying that one day we or those who come after us can expect that, with God's help, the millennium will be established on earth. The millennium remains an eschatological hope. It is located in the future, but it is a future that impacts on the present. Thus we work and pray in the hope of realising the vision. What we succeed in achieving will never fulfil this hope, since the millennium makes all human achievements and institutions provisional. But we cannot slacken in our attempts to realise it – not while God's rule is challenged and his creation suffers.

XIII

The New Jerusalem

John is now ready to show us his vision of the alternative society. He pushes his language and imagery to the limit to show how the new surpasses the old. It is his way of wooing his readers away from the attraction of Babylon.

Then I saw a new heaven and a new earth; for the first heaven and the first earth had passed away, and the sea was no more. And I saw the holy city, the new Jerusalem, coming down out of heaven from God, prepared as a bride adorned for her husband. And I heard a loud voice from the throne saying,

See, the home of God is among mortals.
He will dwell with them;
they will be his peoples,
and God himself will be with them;
he will wipe every tear from their eyes.
Death will be no more;
mourning and crying and pain will be no more,
for the first things have passed away (21.1-4).

This great vision has been the inspiration of hymn writers, artists and city architects. It makes such an impression upon readers that it is easy to be captivated by its beauty and forget the harsh reality which it is intended to challenge.

The vision comes, like so much else in Revelation, from the prophecy of Isaiah (65.17-25) but it is extensively reshaped by John in order to emphasise the magnificence of the new order. John makes it clear that what he is describing is not to be understood as the restoration of a former reality or the transfer to earth of a city pre-existing in heaven. In order to leave us in no doubt as to the radical difference of the new order from the old John tells us that there will be a new heaven and a new earth. He expressly differentiates it from the present order by stating that the first heaven and the first earth have passed away.

One can understand why there should be a new earth when the present earth – the scene of so much hurt and pain – is believed to be corrupt and polluted beyond repair and has to go. But why a new heaven? The answer lies in the fact that in biblical thinking heaven and earth are correlate terms; heaven and earth are all of a piece in ancient thinking (Isa. 51. 6; Ps. 102. 25-26; Matt. 24. 35; 2 Pet. 3. 10). The heaven or the sky was thought of by the ancients as forming a vault or dome to protect the earth (Gen. 1.6-7, Job 37.18). The stars, the sun and moon determine the seasons and the festivals on earth (Gen. 1.14-18). Thus having a newly created earth meant a new heaven to regulate its life.

Further indication of the change in the fortunes promised to those who suffer and cry to God for help is John's statement that "the sea was no more" (21.1). This is the sea, described earlier as set on fire, through which the martyrs have to pass (15.2-4). The sea, like the Beast that emerges from it, symbolises the chaos and evil that have been abolished.

The contrast between the new order and the old is heightened by the description of the New Jerusalem. The city parallels the wretched and putrescent grandeur of Babylon and excels it in significant ways (Gundry, 1987, 254-264). First of all, it is holy (21.2). The cowards, idolaters, and other faithless people who are excluded from the city (21.8) may refer not only to unbelievers but also to Christians who do not have the courage to stand up to the deceptive wiles of the Beast and have succumbed to it. The city is new (21.2). It is part of the new creation. That is to say, it is a completely new phenomenon. Its discontinuity with Babylon is further emphasised by John's statement that it descends out of heaven from God (21.2), i.e., it comes from the newly created heavens. Such a novel idea was nowhere entertained by Jews of the time; they habitually thought of a prototypal city pre-existing in heaven (McKelvey, 1968, 25-41). The prototypal city (like its counterpart on earth) belonged to the old creation ("the first heaven and the first earth"), that in John's scheme of things has been destroyed. His city, like the world order it symbolises, is qualitatively different. Most important of all, the New Jerusalem is "from God" (21.2). It is the gift of God; out of his goodness he gives humanity a new beginning. "The city of God is not the end of human progress. . . . At this end there is found only Babylon" (Ellul, 1977, 214-215). What is needed has been given by God: a new act of creation.

The vision is then ratified and interpreted by God himself. "I heard a loud voice proclaiming from the throne: 'Now God has his dwelling with mankind. He will dwell among them, and they shall be his people' " (21.3 RSV). The New Jerusalem is supremely the place where God is present. Up until this point the presence of God is located in heaven, where the throne is (4.1ff.; etc.). Now it is upon earth. God dwelling with his people echoes the long-held hope of the Jews that ge would one day return to Zion and dwell there again (Ezek.37.27-28; Zech.2.10-11; 8.8). The use of the classic text on the unique relationship established between God and his people based on the covenant ("He will dwell with them and they shall be his people" (21.3 *RSV;* cf. Lev. 26.12) provides the key to what John tells us later about the new city. For the moment he concentrates on showing how this city differs from the city which was responsible for the deaths of so many (18.24). In this city "death will be no more; mourning and crying and pain will be no more" (21.4). The underlying message to the martyrs is again evident: the language used is the same as that used for the blessings promised to the martyrs in 7.17. The reason for the change in the fortunes of those who suffer is explained: "the first things have passed away" (21.4). That is to say, the things that caused pain, sorrow and death were part of the first heaven and the first earth which has been destroyed. Further blessings are to follow, as John will show us presently, because God now dwells on earth.

The introduction to the New Jerusalem is followed by a fuller description. It is the most extensive vision in the whole book, indicating the importance the New Jerusalem holds within the total presentation. All John's rhetorical skills are employed. We need to remind ourselves that what he is describing is a symbolic universe. It is set over against the old order that has been exposed, condemned and destroyed. The superiority of his alternative is symbolised by the design, size, and embellishments of the New Jerusalem and the fact that it is the rendezvous of the nations. John's description uses materials for his city which are drawn from Ezekiel (40-48) and Isaiah (54.11-12; 60.1-22; 61.10; 65.17) and shows an awareness of the New Jerusalem in apocalyptic traditions (Tobit 14.5-7; 4 Ezra 10.44-55; 1 Enoch 90.28-36; Sibylline Oracles 3.702-719; 5.418-433), but it incorporates revolutionary concepts.

The vision first shows us a carefully defined city. It is a compact and clearly demarcated construction. Its design and measurements are symmetrical.

Come, I will show you the bride, the wife of the Lamb'. And in the spirit he carried me away to a great, high mountain and showed me the holy city Jerusalem coming down out of heaven from God. It has the glory of God and a radiance like a very rare jewel, like jasper, clear as crystal. It has a great, high wall with twelve gates, and at the gates twelve angels, and on the gates are inscribed the names of the twelve tribes of the Israelites; on the east three gates, on the north three gates, on the south three gates, and on the west three gates. And the wall of the city has twelve foundations, and on them are the twelve names of the twelve apostles of the Lamb.

The angel who talked to me had a measuring rod of gold to measure the city and its gates and walls. The city lies foursquare, its length the same as its width; and he measured the city with his rod, fifteen hundred miles; its length and width and height are equal. He also measured its wall, one hundred and forty-four cubits by human measurement, which the angel was using" (21.9-17).

By identifying the new Jerusalem as the Bride of the Lamb John indicates that the city symbolises Christ's people. The same thing is signified by the twelve-fold arrangements of the city. Thus its twelve gates bear the names of the twelve tribes and the twelve foundations (i.e. stones of the foundation) have the names of the twelve apostles. Similarly, the city, twelve thousand stadia long, wide and high, is reminiscent of the twelve thousand from each of the twelve tribes. We arrive at the same conclusion if we measure the twelve edges of this extraordinary cubical city: twelve edges of twelve thousand each produce a total of 144,000 (7.1-8; 14.1-5).

The reference is unmistakably to the people of God. The twelve-fold imagery expands on the announcement made in the introduction to the New

Jerusalem in 21.3, which used the Old Testament covenant formula. It sends us back to what John meant earlier when he told us that the twelve tribes were sealed against disaster (7.1-8) and the company of those assembled by the Lamb on Mount Zion numbered 144,000 (14.1-5). John has been preparing his readers for this revelation from the outset. In his letter to the churches he said that those who conquer would bear the name of the New Jerusalem (3.12).

Remarkably, the New Jerusalem has no temple. A city without a temple would have been inconceivable to the ancients. How then did John make this daring break with tradition? The answer very likely lies in his compelling desire to show the innovative character of the new order. Commentators believe that John was preparing his readers for this novelty when he told them that the New Jerusalem was, surprisingly, cubiform (21.16). The explanation for this architectural phenomenon is debated by scholars (McKelvey 171-178). It is most likely to be found in the description of the holy of holies in the temple in Jerusalem as cubical (1 Kings 6.20; cf. Mishnah, *Middoth* 4.6, with reference to the whole sanctuary). What John appears to be saying is that the New Jerusalem is all temple. The enormous size of the city is a hint as to the meaning of the imagery. Fifteen hundred miles is roughly the distance from Patmos to London. Not only so, the city is equally high! What John must mean is that the city is one great temple. But the circumscribed character of the imagery does not permit us to go so far as to say that the city is coextensive with the universe. This becomes clearer as the vision unfolds.

More surprises are in store for us. Just when we thought we had made sense of the symbolism of the New Jerusalem the images change before our eyes. Instead of the cube-like construction we see an enormous sprawling metropolis, so enormous in fact that it is capable of accommodating all the nations of the earth. This transposition of images indicates that the New Jerusalem is no longer a symbol simply of the people of God. The emphasis now is not on a closely defined group (the 144000), but on inclusiveness.

The nations will walk by its light, and the kings of the earth will bring their glory into it. Its gates will never be shut by day – and there will be no night there. People will bring into it the glory and the honour of the nations. But nothing unclean will enter it, nor anyone who practices abomination or falsehood, but only those who are written in the Lamb's book of life (21.24-27).

The shift from the particularism signified by the carefully defined cube to the universalism of an enormous international city, whose gates are permanently open to receive all who wish to enter, has puzzled commentators. What contradiction is it that peoples the new world with nations who come to the New Jerusalem for salvation? Did they not perish along with the old world? It seems that John's imagination has got the better of him or that an editor has hopelessly confused the vision. Neither in fact is the case. What we have here is something that runs through the entire Bible: it is the tension between the particular and the universal, i.e., between the people of God and the nations at large. We were introduced to this in chapter 7, where alongside the sharply delineated company of the 144,000 we had the vision of the multitude so huge that it could not be counted.

John's picture of the nations going about their business in the light that radiates from the New Jerusalem and taking their tribute into it means that the new world has people who need converting (cf. the healing of the nations in 22.2). Evidently the city, though of vast dimensions, does not cover the whole of the earth and the nations are thought of as living outside it, as are the unclean and those who practise abomination and falsehood (22.15). The ever-open gates of the New Jerusalem stand for the evangelical calling of God's people, who are now "a great multitude that no one could count, from every nation, from all tribes and peoples and languages" (7.9). As Bauckham points out, "the universalism of the vision of the New Jerusalem completes the direction towards the conversion of the nations which was already clearly indicated in 11.13; 14.14-16; 15.4" (1993b, 139).

The significance of John's statement that "the kings of the earth" bring their tribute into the New Jerusalem is that these are the client rulers who were formerly in league with Rome and thus opposed to God (6.15; 17.2, 18; 18.3, 9; 19.19; Caird, 279; Bauckham, 1993b, 315). Similarly, the nations who bring their tribute to the New Jerusalem (21.24-26) were once intoxicated and exploited by Rome (14.8; 17.2; 18.3). "The glory and the honour of the nations" are voluntarily brought into this city (Caird, 279; Bauckham 1993b, 315).

The evangelical message of John's vision of the new age is again in evidence in his statement that the leaves of the tree of life are for "the healing of the nations" (22.2):

> Then the angel showed me the river of the water of life, bright as crystal, flowing from the throne of God and of the Lamb through the middle of the street of the city. On either side of the river, is the tree of life with its twelve kinds of fruit, producing its fruit each month; and the leaves of the tree are for the healing of the nations. Nothing accursed will be found there any more. But the throne of God and of the Lamb will be in it, and his servants will worship him; they will see his face, and his name will be on their foreheads. And there will be no more night; they need no light of lamp or sun, for the Lord God will be their light, and they will reign for ever and ever (22.1-5).

The vision has changed again. What began as a blueprint for the construction of the New Jerusalem and then focused on people streaming into the city to worship God now points to the quality of life in the new age. The New Jerusalem is a place of light (21.24). The nations find salvation in it and direct their policies according to its guidance (21.24). Unlike earthly cities the gates of this city do not need to be shut for there is nothing to cause harm (21.27). It is a place of life, vitality and great fecundity (22.1-2). Particularly striking is John's adaptation of Ezekiel's images (47.1-12).

It expands on Ezekiel (47.1), describing the river as "the water of life", i.e., life-giving (cf. John 7.38), and by increasing the variety of fruits on the tree(s) and telling us that the leaves of the tree(s) are not simply for healing, but for the healing of the oppressed and oppressing nations.

Most important of all is the presence in this city of the symbol of justice and righteousness: the throne of God and of the Lamb (22.1, 3). It is for this reason that the new age is most aptly described in terms of Paradise. When God dwells on earth there is peace and plenty. There is no danger. What is more, everyone now enjoys access to God. Those who stand before the throne in worship experience the greatest blessing John could conceive of: seeing God face to face and enjoying his salvation (22.4-5).

In terms of John's purpose in writing his book, the most expressive part of the vision comes at the very end and connects with the millennium vision; it is the throne of God and of the Lamb set up on earth (22.1, 3). What those who risk their lives in witnessing to truth and justice are promised is not an escape into a heavenly world but life on a renewed earth. The faithful are not taken up into the New Jerusalem; it comes down to them. It is planted firmly upon this earth. It is no exaggeration to say that the whole point of John's writing his book is to impress upon his readers the fact that it is *this* world which is the place where God's righteousness will triumph. Like the Jewish apocalyptic writers who laboured to challenge tyrannical regimes and sustain the faith of the persecuted, John never allows evil and suffering, however grievous, to cause him to give up hope for the world. He resolutely affirms his belief that people will dwell on earth and live without fear of evil or want. But John's hope has a different axis from the Jewish writers. It is based upon Jesus Christ and his victory. Thus he moves his readers onwards from his opening vision of the throne of God to his closing vision of the throne of God and of the Lamb. Between these foci is the vision of the Lamb that was slain, now raised to life. Thus from the vindication and resurrection of Christ we pass to the vindication and resurrection of the martyrs. John is thus at one with the apostle Paul in making the resurrection of the body the pledge of the new creation (Rom. 8.23).

How we are to envisage the new earth defies the imagination. It is metaphor. What it stands for is of the greatest possible significance in determining the values by which Christians are to live and to which they are called to bear witness. It does not provide us with answers to the vexing social and political problems of our times, but by showing us that the material world is of fundamental importance to God it does indicate that finding answers to such questions should be our concern.

The place the earth occupies in the vision of the New Jerusalem links it with the millennium. Other connections are made by those commentators who believe that the New Jerusalem depicts the glories of the millennium (Mealy, 47-52). The paradisiacal nature of the new age is taken to be a description of the millennium, and a direct reference to the millennium is found in the statement that the inhabitants of the New Jerusalem "will reign forever and ever" (22.5). However, the use of the New Jerusalem vision to interpret the millennium is ruled out by a number of things. As we saw, there is a very definite break between the account of the millennium in chapter 20 and the description of the New Jerusalem in chapters 21-22. John could not have made it clearer that chapter 21 introduces a wholly new order of things. What is more, the millennium is the reward of those who suffer martyrdom, whereas the New Jerusalem is for all.

John's vision ends with the New Jerusalem and the new heaven and the new earth. What follows is an epilogue concerned largely with the origin and authority of his writing (22.6-21). Included in this section is the hope of the return of Jesus Christ (22.7, 12,20). This picks up the earlier references to the Second Coming (1.7; 2.16; 3.3, 11; 16.15). John thus shares with New Testament writers generally the belief in the imminent return of Christ. The problem posed by the delay of the Parousia which we find already expressed within the New Testament (2 Thess. 2.1-12; 2 Pet. 3.1-13) has been the subject of a great deal of scholarly attention and need not concern us here. As we saw, the Second Coming is not connected with the millennium and the New Jerusalem. The latter stand in their own right. John's visions of cosmic catastrophe should not be taken to mean the end of the world. Although John expected the Second Coming, he does not tell us anything about it, apart from expecting it to happen soon. But however he conceived of it, the future he has in mind is upon this earth. That is his primary interest. That is where he wishes his readers to concentrate their efforts.

XIV
Conclusion

The approach of the year 2000 invites us to look at what the Book of Revelation says about the millennium and its meaning for today. For too long the subject has been neglected if not ignored. Or the millennium has been made an appendage to the Second Coming. Or it has been historicised and taken to mean an earthly paradise, whose non-fulfilment has resulted in bitter disappointment, ignominy and ridicule. It is time to state clearly and unequivocally that the millennium is a metaphor. It symbolises God's triumph over evil in the person of Jesus Christ and the vindication of the victims of oppression and injustice. It is a promise we are to expect to see realised upon earth; it relates to how we live in the here and now, but at the same time it is a transcendent eschatological hope which will not be realised until God consummates all things. Although we should not make the fatal mistake of taking the millennium hope literally and invest earthly instit-utions or movements with an exclusive and final authority, when they should be regarded as historically conditioned and provisional, we should work and pray for the realisation of what the millennium represents.

It cannot be too strongly emphasised that the millennium hope is a hope for this world, and not a denial of the world or retreat from it. It stands for the defeat of fatalism and despair of the world and points us to new possibil-ities. It gives us hope so that we do not accept that things need to be the way they are, that they cannot be changed and that all is ultimately meaningless. It will not allow us to underestimate the power of evil and its ability to crush us, but it assures us that in the battle between good and evil the victory ultimately will go to truth and goodness. It points us to the vision of a new heaven and a new earth. The millennium is thus an essential element of the Christian hope.

From the perspective of John's vision we are in a position to understand the strengths and weaknesses of the millenarian movements which have appeared in history. As we saw in the earlier part of this study, these move-ments fall into two main categories: world-affirming and world-denying.

First and foremost, the millennium vision is the pledge that God cares for the life of his people upon earth and matters of human allegiance, truth and justice are his concern. It is in this world that God's cause will be vindi-cated and the faithful will experience his blessing. Whatever should be said about the fanaticism and the destructive consequences of movements like the Taborites, Thomas Müntzer and his New Jerusalem, the Anabaptists and the Fifth Monarchy Men, we have to give them the credit for setting out to address the wrongs suffered by the poor and the oppressed. They believed that they were called by the righteous God to make the earth a righteous place. But their strength was also their weakness and the cause of their downfall. In their well-intentioned eagerness to put down evil and relieve the downtrodden they took the Bible literally and turned the millennium into a political ideology. Divine authority was claimed for secular power and bred new horrors. In similar fashion, when the church believed itself to be the embodiment of the millennium it became triumphalist and had no hesitation in using secular power to enforce conformity to what it believed was God's will. In both cases the millennial hope lost its transcendent and eschatological character. It no longer served as a critique of existing beliefs and institutions.

An attempt to express the transcendent and eschatological character of the biblical millennium is found in presentations of the End which link the millennium with the Second Coming. In an age that was in danger of losing contact with reality through being carried away by romantic Enlightenment beliefs in the invincibility of progress and moral betterment, the Parousia was seen to call in question all facile hopes and offer a more realistic view of the world. But once again what was the source of their strength became the cause of their weakness. Adventist teaching often resulted in an ambivalent attitude towards earthly endeavours and human reforms. The world was seen as growing increasingly evil and beyond human help. Its only hope was Christ's return. Christ returns to earth, not to help his people in their battle against evil, not to challenge evil, but to rescue the faithful from it. The more world-denying movements have the millennium taking place not on earth but in heaven or postponed until the advent of the new heaven and the new earth.

Only a middle course preserving both the transcendent, eschatological and earthly character of the millennium can hope to do justice to John's vision. Its transcendent dimension is particularly necessary in an age in which faith in God, or in God as providentially directing the world, is questioned. It is significant that before John says a thing about the church's task in the world or deals with the future he directs our attention to God – God and the Lamb ruling our chaotic world and worshipped by the hosts of heaven and earth. John's vision of the slain Lamb at the heart of God's throne is the key to making God real for ourselves and our contemporaries. In and through Christ God is involved in our world, bringing good out of evil. As we allow John's example of never thinking of God without thinking of Christ to influence our worship and reflection, the task of making connections between our faith and our world becomes less difficult. Similarly, the Christological understanding of God preserves the eschatological character of the millennium. The victory of the Lamb is the victory of God. The slain Lamb raised to life is the harbinger of the resurrection of the just, and the millennium a preview of the new creation. The eschatological millennium thus saves us from despairing of the world or regarding the *status quo* as inevitable or satisfactory. It is of particular relevance to an age that finds it difficult even to think about the future.

The terrestrial nature of the millennium is linked to the rhetorical and practical purpose with which John writes. Revelation thus helps us not only to clarify the issues, but to see what the consequences are for us. As soon as it has shown us the new world it calls for commitment and action on the part of its readers. Readers today live in a different context from John's, but when they pray "Thy Kingdom come, thy will be done on earth" they cannot evade the challenge of translating John's message for a world which is rampant with idolatry and injustice.

It would be surprising if in making the connection between our world and John's alternative world our response did not begin where John believed his contemporaries should begin, viz. with a change of heart and mind. When we find that the causes of our crisis today lie in human selfishness, sin and idolatry, our primary and inescapable need is to repent and realign our living so that we are centred on God and God's concern for the wretched of the earth. Nor is there any way of escaping the fact that translating John's vision for today's world will result in a determined resolve to bring the gospel to bear upon the idolatries of our time and their disastrous consequences and work to remove wrongs and promote life-enhancing initiatives. The millennium and the New Jerusalem are not only hope for the future, but an agenda for the present.

BIBLIOGRAPHY

Aagaard, Johannes, *Mission, Konfession, Kirche: die Problematik ihrer Integration im 19. Jahrhundert in Deutschland,* Copenhagen: Gleerups, 1967.

Alexander, P.S., "The Family of Caesar and the Family of God: The Image of the Emperor in the Heikhalot Literature," *Images of Empire,* ed. L. Alexander, Sheffield: Sheffield Academic Press, 1991, 276-297.

Aune, David E., "The Influence of Roman Imperial Court Ceremonial on the Apocalypse of John", *Journal of the Chicago Society of Biblical Research* XXVIII (1983), 5-26.

Aune, David E., "Following the Lamb: Discipleship in the Apocalypse", in *Patterns of Discipleship in the New Testament,* Richard N. Longenecker, ed., Grand Rapids, Michigan/Cambridge UK: W. B. Eerdmans, 1996.

Aune, David E., *Revelation 1-5* and *Revelation 6-16,* Word Biblical Commentary, Dallas: Word Books 1997, 1998.

Barker, Margaret, *The Risen Lord,* Edinburgh: T. & T. Clark, 1996.

Barkum, M., *Crucible of the Millennium,* Syracuse, New York: Syracuse University Press, 1986.

Bauckham, Richard, *The Bible in Politics,* London: SPCK, 1989.

Bauckham, Richard, *The Climax of Prophecy: Studies on the Book of Revelation,* Edinburgh: T. & T. Clark, 1993a.

Bauckham, Richard, *The Theology of the Book of Revelation,* Cambridge: Cambridge University Press, 1993b.

Beasley-Murray, G.R., *The Book of Revelation,* London: Oliphants, 1974.

Bietenhard, H., "The Millennial Hope in the Early Church", *Scottish Journal of Theology* 6 (1953), 12-30.

Bloch, Ruth H., *Visionary Republic: Millennial Themes in American Thought,* 1756-1800, Cambridge: Cambridge University Press, 1985.

Bloomfield, M. and Reeves, M., "The Penetration of Joachimism into Northern Europe", *Speculum,* 29 (1954), 772-793.

Boesak, Allan A., *Comfort and Protest: Reflections on the Apocalypse of John of Patmos,* Edinburgh: St. Andrew Press, 1987.

Bogue, D. and Bennett, J., *History of Dissenters from the Revolution in 1688 to the year 1808,* London: Williams & Smith, 4 vols., 1808-1812.

Bosch, David J. *Transforming Mission: Paradigm Shifts in Theology of Mission,* Maryknoll, New York: Orbis Books, 1991.

Brailsford, N.N., *The Levellers and the English Revolution,* ed. Christopher Hill, London: The Crescent Press, 1961.

Breders, A.H., *Christendom and Christianity in the Middle Ages,* Grand Rapids: William B. Eerdmans, 1984.

Broughton, T.R.S., *"Asia Minor under the Empire, 27B.C.-A.D.337",* in T. Frank (ed.), *An Economic Survey of Ancient Rome,* Baltimore: John Hopkins Press, IV, 1938, 593-902.

Caird, George B., *A Commentary on the Revelation of St. John the Divine,*

London: A. & C. Black, 1966.

Caird, George B., *The Language and Imagery of the Bible,* London: Duckworth, 1980.

Capp, Philip L., "Eschatology: its Relevance to Mission from an Evangelical Perspective", *Missionalia* 15 (1987), 110-118.

Carey, William, *An Enquiry into the Obligations of Christians to use Means for the Conversion of the Heathens,* Leicester, 1792.

Chandler, Russell, *Doomsday*, Milton Keynes, 1993.

Chaney, Charles L., *The Birth of Missions in America,* Pasadena: William Carey Library, 1976.

Charles, R.H., *A Critical and Exegetical Commentary on the Revelation of St. John*, 2 vols, Edinburgh: T&T Clark, 1920.

Clouse, Robert G., "Johann Heinrich Alsted and English Millennialism", *Harvard Theological Review* 62 (1969), 189-207.

Clouse, Robert G., *The Meaning of the Millennium*, ed., Illinois: Inter Varsity Press, 1979.

Clouse, Robert G., *New 20th Century Encyclopedia of Religious Knowledge*, Grand Rapids: Baker Book House, 2nd. edit., 1991, 561-562.

Clouse, Robert G., *Evangelical Dictionary of Theology,* Grand Rapids and Carlisle: Baker Books and Paternoster Press, 1984, 714-718.

Cohn, Norman, *The Pursuit of the Millennium*, London: Secker and Warburg, 1957.

Collins, Adela Yarbro, *The Combat Myth in the Book of Revelation,* Missoula: Scholars Press, 1976.

Collins, Adela Yarbro, *The Apocalypse*, Dublin: Veritas Publications, 1979.

Collins, Adela Yarbro, *Crisis and Catharsis: The Power of the Apocalypse*, Philadelphia: The Westminster Press, 1984.

Darby, J.N., *Collected Works,* ed. William Kelly, Kingston-on-Thames: Stow Hill Bible and Tract Depot, 1960.

De Jong, J.A., *As the Waters Cover the Sea: Millennial Expectations in the Rise of Anglo-American Missions 1640-1810,* Kampen: Kok, 1970.

Dodge G.H., *The Political Theory of the Huguenots of the Dispersion, with Special Reference to the Thought and Influence of Pierre Jurieu,* New York and London: 1947.

Edwards, J. *Apocalyptic Writings*, ed. Stephen T. Stein, New Haven and London: Yale University Press, 1977.

Ellacuria, I. and J.Sobrino, *Mysterium Liberationis: Fundamental Concepts of Liberation Theology,* ed., Maryknoll, New York: Orbis Books, 1993.

Ellul, J., *The Book of Revelation*, trans. G.W. Schreiner, New York: Seabury Press, 1977.

Festinger, L., *A Theory of Cognitive Dissonance,* London: Tavistock, 1962.

Fiorenza, Elisabeth Schüssler, *The Book of Revelation: Justice and Judgment*, Philadelphia: Fortress Press, 1985.

Flint, Valerie I.J., *The Imaginative Landscape of Christopher Columbus*, Princeton, New Jersey: Princeton University Press, 1992.

Ford, J.M., *Revelation*, Garden City, New York: Doubleday & Co., 1975.

France, J., *Rodulfus Glaber Opera,* Oxford: The Clarendon Press, 1989.

Garrett, Clarke, *Respectable Folly: Millenarians and the French Revolution in*

France and England, Baltimore and London: John Hopkins Press, 1975.

Garrow, A.J.P., *Revelation,* London: Routledge, 1997.

Giblin, Charles Homer, "Recapitulation and the Literary Coherence of John's Apocalypse", *Catholic Biblical Quarterly* 56, (1994) 81-95.

Gilbertson, Michael, *The Meaning of the Millennium,* Cambridge: Grove Books Ltd., 1997.

Glaber, Rodulfus. *Rodulfus Glaber Opera,* trans. by J. France, Oxford: Clarendon Press, 1989.

Goertz, H.-J., *The Anabaptists,* London and New York: Routledge, 1996.

Good News of the Kingdom, Watchtower Bible and Tract Society, Brooklyn, New York, 1982.

Gundry, Robert H., "The New Jerusalem: People Not Place", *Novum Testamentum* 29 (1987), 254-264.

Gutiérrez, G., *Theology of Liberation, History, Politics and Salvation,* London: SCM Press, 1974.

Hanegraaff, Wouter J. *New Age Religion and Western Culture: Esotericism in the Mirror of Secular Thought,* Leiden, New York and Köln: E.J. Brill 1996.

Hanson, Paul D., *The Dawn of Apocalyptic: the Historical and Sociological Roots of Jewish Apocalyptic Eschatology,* Philadelphia: Fortress Press, 1979.

Harrison, J.F.C., *The Second Coming: Popular Millenarianism 1780-1850,* London: Routledge and Kegan Paul, 1979.

Hemer, Colin J., *The Letters to the Seven Churches of Asia in their Local Setting,* Sheffield: Sheffield Academic Press, 1986.

Hill, Christopher, *The World Upside Down: Radical Ideas during the English Revolution,* Middlesex: Penguin Books, 1974.

Hobsbawn, Eric, *Primitive Rebels, Studies in Archaic Forms of Social Movement in the 19th and 20th Centuries,* reprinted edit. New York: W.W. Norton and Co. 1965.

Hopkins, Charles Howard, *The Rise of the Social Gospel in American Protestantism, 1865-1915,* New Haven: Yale University Press, 1940.

Hubback, A., *The Prophets of Doom: The Security Threat of Religious Cults,* Institute for European Defence and Strategic Studies, Alliance Publications, 1996.

Kraybill, J. Nelson, *Imperial Cult and Commerce in John's Apocalypse,* Sheffield, Sheffield Academic Press, 1996.

Kyle, Richard, *Awaiting the Millennium,* Leicester: Inter-Varsity Press, 1998.

Lindsey, Hal, with C.C. Carlson, *The Late Great Planet Earth,* Grand Rapids: Zondervan, 1970.

Lindsay, Hal, *The 1980s: Countdown to Armageddon,* Basingstoke: Lakeland, 1981.

Lindsey, Hal, *Planet Earth – 2000 AD: Will Mankind Survive?,* Palos Verdes, California: Western Front, 1994.

Lovett, R., *History of the London Missionary Society,* I, London: Henry Frowde, 1899.

Luther, Martin, *Works,* Philadelphia: Muhlenberg Press, 1955-1986.

Marshall, I.H., "Martyrdom and Parousia in the Revelation of John", *Studia Evangelica* 4 (1968), 333-339.

Matheson, P., *The Collective Works of Thomas Müntzer,* ed. Edinburgh: T. & T.

Clark, 1988.

Mealy, J.Webb, *After the Thousand Years: Resurrection and Judgement in Revelation 20*, Sheffield: Sheffield Academic Press, 1992.

Metz, Johann Baptist, *Theology of the World*, New York, Herder & Herder, 1969.

McGinn, Bernard, *Visions of the End: Apocalyptic Traditions in the Middle Ages,* New York: Columbia University Press, 1979.

McGinn, Bernard, *The Calabrian Abbot: Joachim of Fiore in the History of Western Thought*, New York: Macmillan, 1985.

McKelvey, R.J., *The New Temple,* Oxford: Oxford University Press, 1968.

Moltmann, Jürgen, *The Theology of Hope,* London: SCM Press, 1967.

Moltmann, Jürgen, *The Coming of God*: *Christian Eschatology*, London: SCM Press, 1996.

Murray, Ian, *The Puritan Hope: A Study in Revival and the Interpretation of Scripture*, London: Banner of Truth Trust, 1971.

O'Leary, S.D., *Arguing the Apocalypse: A Theory of Millennial Rhetoric,* New York and Oxford: Oxford University Press, 1994.

Pawson, David, *When Jesus Returns,* London etc.: Hodder & Stoughton, 1995.

Penton, M. James, *Apocalypse Delayed: The Story of Jehovah's Witnesses*, Toronto: University of Toronto Press, 1985.

Phelan, J.L., *The Millennium Kingdom of the Franciscans in the New World*, Berkeley and Los Angeles, 1970.

Pocock, Michael, "The Destiny of the World and the Work of Missions", *Bibliotheca Sacra*, 145 (1988), 436-451.

Reddish, Mitchell G., "Martyr Christology in the Apocalypse", *Journal for the Study of the New Testament,* 33 (1988), 85-95.

Reeves M., *Joachim of Fiore and the Prophetic Future*, London: SPCK, 1976.

Revelation of Ramala (anonymous), Saffron Walden: C.W. Daniel Co., 1976.

Robinson, J.A.T., *Redating the New Testament,* London: SCM Press, 1976.

Rogers, P.G., *The Fifth Monarchy Men*, London: Oxford University Press, 1966.

Rostovtzeff, Mihail, *The Social and Economic History of the Roman Empire*, 2 vols. 2ed., Revised by P.M. Fraser, Oxford: Clarendon Press, 1957.

Rowland, Christopher, *Revelation*, London: Epworth Press, 1993.

Russell, Charles Taze, *Thy Kingdom Come*, Brooklyn: New York, 1926.

Sandeen, E.R., *The Roots of Fundamentalism,* Chicago: University of Chicago Press, 1970.

Schäufele, Wolfgang, *Das Missionarische Bewusstsein und Wirken der Taufer,* Neukirchen-Vluyn: Verlag des Erziehungsvereins, 1960.

Segundo, J.L., *The Liberation of Theology*, Dublin: Gill and Macmillan, 1977.

Sobrino, J., "Central Position of the Reign of God in Liberation Theology", *Mysterium Liberationis: Fundamental Concepts of Liberation Theology,* ed. I. Ellacuria and J. Sobrino, Maryknoll, New York, Orbis Books, 1993, 350-388.

St. Clair, M.J., *Millennium Movements in Historical Context,* New York: Garland, 1992.

Sweet, John, *Revelation*, London: SCM, 1979.

Swete, Henry Barclay, *The Apocalypse of St. John*, London: Macmillan and Co., 1906.

Talmon, Y., "Pursuit of the Millennium: The Relationship between Religious and Social Change", *Archives européennes de sociologie* 7 (1966),159-200.

Talmon, Y., "Millenarianism", *International Encyclopedia of the Social Sciences*, ed. D.L. Sills, New York: Free Press, 1968.

Thomas, Norman, ed., *Readings in Mission*, London: SPCK, 1995.

Thompson, Damian, *The End of Time,* London: Minerva, 1997.

Thompson, Leonard L., *The Book of Revelation: Apocalypse and Empire*, New York and Oxford: Oxford University Press, 1990.

Toon, Peter, *Puritans, The Millennium and the Future of Israel: Puritan Eschatology 1600-1660*, Cambridge and London: James Clarke & Co., 1970.

Trevelyan, George, *A Vision of the Aquarian Age*, London: Coventure, 1979.

Tuveson, E.L., *Millennium and Utopia: A Study in the Background of the Idea of Progress*, New York: Harper and Row, 1964.

Wainwright, Arthur W., *Mysterious Apocalypse: Interpreting the Book of Revelation,* Nashville: Abingdon Press, 1993.

Walker, Andrew, *Restoring the Kingdom: the Radical Christianity of the House Church Movement,* Guildford, Surrey: Eagle, 2nd edit. 1998.

Watts, Pauline Moffitt, "Prophecy and Discovery: On the Spiritual Origins of Christopher Columbus's 'Enterprise of the Indies'", *American Historical Review* 90 (1985), 73-102.

Wengst, Klaus, *Pax Romana and the Peace of Jesus Christ,* London: SCM, 1987.

White, R.F., "Reexamining the Evidence for Recapitulation in Revelation 20:1-10", *Westminster Theological Journal* 51 (1989), 319-344.

Worsley, Peter, *The Trumpet Shall Sound: A Study of "Cargo" Cults in Melanesia*, London: MacGibbon and Kee, 1957.

Subject Index

TEXT INDEX

OLD TESTAMENT

NEW TESTAMENT

APOCRYPHA

JEWISH PSEUDEPIGRAPHA

DEAD SEA SCROLLS

1 QH11 (3).3-18   66

RABBINIC LITERATURE

Mishnah
Yoma
3.6   64
7.4   64

Middoth
4.6   88

Talmud
b Sanhedrin
99a   82

Heikhalot Lit 60

CLASSICAL LITERATURE

Aelius Aristides
Oratio 11   73

Juvenal
Satires
8.87-90   73

Petronius
Satyricum
119   73

Pliny the Elder
Natural History
37.204   73

Pliny the Younger
Epistles
10.96,97   48

Tacitus
Annals
1.10.4   73

Virgil
Georgics
1.56-59   73

EARLY CHURCH WRITERS

Augustine
City of God
20.7-17   14

Origen
De Principiis
2.11.2   14

Irenaeus
Against Heresies
5.32   13

Justin Martyr
Dialogue
80-81   13

Tertullian
Against Marcion
3.25   14

NAME INDEX

Aagaard, J. 26, 27
Aelius Aristides 73
Alexander, P.S. 60
Alsted, J.H. 18, 19
Anabaptists 17, 23, 26
Asahara, S. 38-39
Asia Minor 47, 48, 49, 53-55, 72-73
Augustine 7, 10, 14, 19
Aquarius 39-40
Aum Shinrikyo 38-39, 40
Aune, D.E. 8, 50, 57, 69

Baptist Missionary Society 25
Barker, M. 58
Barkum, M. 35
Barnabas 13
Bauckham, R. 8, 10, 47, 49, 53, 73, 74-75, 82, 89
Bengel, J.A. 26
Bennett, J. 22
Bietenhard, H. 13, 14
Bloch, R.H. 21, 29
Bloomfield, M. 16
Boesak, A.A. 74
Bogue, D. 22, 25
Bosch, D.J. 32
Brailsford, N.N. 19
Branch Davidians 38
Breders, A.H. 15
Broughton, T.R.S. 54
Burder, G. 25

Caird, G.B. 58, 64, 65, 74, 78, 89
Calvin, J. 18
Capp, P.L. 28
Carey, W. 25
Cayce, E 39
Chandler, R. 37
Chaney, C.L. 27
Charles, R.H. 83
Cho, D.Y. 37
Church Missionary Society 25, 26
Clouse, R.G. 18
Cohn, N. 15, 17, 22, 23
Collins, A.Y. 8, 66
Columbus, C. 14, 16-17, 24
Commodianus 13
Constantine 14

Cromwell, O. 20
Crompton, R. 35

Darby, J.N. 33-34
da Gama, V. 24
Diggers 19
Diocletian 60
de Jong, J.A. 25, 26, 28
Dodge, G.H. 21
Domitian 48, 57

Edwards, J. 20, 27
Ellacuria, I. 30
Ellul, J. 72, 86

Festinger, L. 41
Fiorenza, E.S. 8
Flint, V.I.J. 16
Ford, J.M. 56
France, J. 15
Franciscans 16, 24-25
Freytag, W. 29

Garrett, C. 21
Garrow, A.J.P. 67
Giblin, C.H. 50
Gilbertson, M. 13
Glaber 15
Glasgow Missionary Society 26
Goertz, H-J. 17
Gundry, R.H. 86

Hamilton, A. 18
Hanegraaff, W.J. 39
Hanson, P.D. 46
Harrison, J.F.C. 20
Hemer, C.J. 67
Hill, C. 19
Hippolytus 13
Hobsbawn, E. 22
Hofmann, M. 26
Hopkins, C.H. 35
Hopkins, S. 27
Horne, M. 26
Hubback, A. 40
Huss, J. 17

Ignatius 48